A Quid without Any Quo

A Quid without Any Quo

—— Gospel Freedom according to Galatians ——

BY

Jason Micheli

FOREWORDS BY

Ken Jones
&
Will Willimon

CASCADE *Books* · Eugene, Oregon

Cascade Books
An Imprint of Wipf and Stock Publishers
199 W. 8th Ave., Suite 3
Eugene, OR 97401

www.wipfandstock.com

PAPERBACK ISBN: 978-1-6667-4450-7
HARDCOVER ISBN: 978-1-6667-4451-4
EBOOK ISBN: 978-1-6667-4452-1

Cataloguing-in-Publication data:

Names: Micheli, Jason, author. | Jones, Ken, 1946–, foreword. | Willimon, William H., foreword.

Title: A Quid without any quo : gospel freedom according to Galatians / by Jason Micheli ; forewords by Ken Jones and Will Willimon.

Description: Eugene, OR : Cascade Books, 2023 | Includes bibliographical references.

Identifiers: ISBN 978-1-6667-4450-7 (paperback) | ISBN 978-1-6667-4451-4 (hardcover) | ISBN 978-1-6667-4452-1 (ebook)

Subjects: LCSH: Bible.—Galatians—Commentaries.

Classification: BS2685.53 .M52 2023 (print) | BS2685.53 .M52 (ebook)

07/20/23

To Fleming, mentor and muse

Contents

Foreword by Ken Jones | ix
Foreword by Will Willimon | xiii

A Quid without Any Quo | 1
God-Damned Preachers | 9
Apocalypto | 17
All You Need Is Nothing | 26
Cheapened Grace | 34
Lay Your Deadly Doing Down | 42
The Sin-Eater | 50
The Power of Positive Blaming | 57
Critical Grace Theory | 65
With the Grain of the Universe | 73
Walking into Speech | 82
Verification Principle | 91
Live Their Worst Life Now | 99
Cruciform Calisthenics | 106

Bibliography | 115

Foreword

By Ken Jones

T HE TWENTY-CENTURY MARRIAGE BETWEEN God's word and the church has been a rocky one. It's reminiscent of the God-arranged marriage between the Old Testament prophet Hosea and the prostitute Gomer. It was a marriage that produced children named Unloved and No-Relation. By the end of the prophet's speech, though, God declares, "I will betroth you in faithfulness, and you will acknowledge the Lord."

There are all kinds of things you might assume about this marriage from the outside, but Paul's Letter to the Galatians gives us an insider's look at what happens when a divine word both judges and loves sinners into freedom and new life. Galatians is sort of a day-in-the-life marital snapshot. It's a moment of vivid truth-telling when the gentile Galatians show themselves equal to the Israelites in faithlessness, even as they serve as predictors of our own stance in regard to God's promise in Christ.

An honest reader of Galatians is forced into a self-reckoning. Paul calls the gentile converts away from a slide into faithlessness that would result in a devastating breach with God. It's judgment and he's purple-faced angry. No doubt about that. But he never lets them forget the promise of Jesus' own faithfulness that claimed them in the first place. He's a damn fine couples counselor.

For us to experience the shock and relief that comes in an encounter with Galatians requires more than simply words on a page. Cleopas and his pal on the way to Emmaus had the text of the Old Testament well in hand, yet they still couldn't grasp what the events of Passover in Jerusalem meant. They needed the well-disguised Jesus they met roadside to make sense of it. In other words, even mere hours after the women returned from the empty tomb, the faith of the Emmaus travelers required interpretation. Jesus was the first preacher of the gospel. If the span of a few hours and days after Christ's death and resurrection already showed the need for biblical commentary, how much more do we need help making a 2,000-year-old text come alive?

The Reformation catchphrase *sola scriptura* has often been seen as a demand for freedom from a magisterium established to tell us how to interpret the Bible. But that wasn't the intent of Martin Luther and his fellow evangelical preachers and teachers. "Word alone" means the word is powerful enough to create faith. When God's judgment and gracious promises are let loose, it becomes explosive on the order of Pentecost morning. With Galatians the problem is that the fog of those intervening centuries makes it extraordinarily difficult to hear this word with the auditory clarity of the letter's initial recipients in central Turkey.

Jason Micheli makes quick work of this millennia-spanning task, because he is first and foremost a deft preacher whose weekly climbs into the pulpit have resulted in years of prime proclamation of the gospel. He regularly begins with those words on the page and then does an *omnium gatherum*, a pulling together of literary erudition, connections to popular culture, a deep awareness of his own and the rest of humanity's brokenness, and an intimate knowledge of the broad arc of the biblical story. Sunday after Sunday he finds a way to weave it all together in a manner that makes the Holy Spirit a bit less in need of a postworship Sunday afternoon nap.

This brief commentary revels in letting us see its homiletical underwear. It's born in the pulpit and shows us what Paul meant and means still. But it also serves as an antidote to the kind of preaching that offers up an arid litany of facts culled from commentaries. It's a primer for how to preach. Micheli has bigger fish to fry than the usual biblical *kommentariat*: lengthier run-of-the-mill Galatians commentaries offer guppies of historical tidbits, but this one cooks up a swordfish filet that more closely resembles what happened between Jerusalem and Emmaus.

Micheli doesn't just give an account of what happened way back when. He consistently seeks to provide the same *quid* without a *quo* that Paul did. In each chapter he pours a 200-proof gospel, straight-no-chaser. Freedom with *no* strings attached. What happens in these pages holds the possibility of a person saying, "God, this is the strangest heartburn. Ever. I didn't know I could be this free."

What Cleopas and his pal heard, what the uncircumcised believers in Galatia got from Paul, and what we have here provides us a promise bigger than millennia of commentaries, millions of faithless sinners, and masses of letters on a page. We have this one true thing: God has done the reckoning, and the accounts are cleared. We can quit the *quid pro quo* bargaining and enjoy a freedom in this marriage that's lasting and free.

Foreword

By Will Willimon

J ASON MICHELI IS A good enough Bible scholar and theologian to know that Paul's letter to the Galatians is a bomb planted in the middle of the church. In this book, Jason as pastor and preacher is reckless enough to light the fuse.

Jason is not only a fine writer (cancer is funny, marriage is living in sin?) and an engaging preacher (one commentator said that listening to Jason is like drinking water from a fire hose), he is also one of our best Christologically informed readers of scripture.

Keep ever before you, as you read this book, that it's written by a Methodist, a pastor of a denomination that unashamedly took as its slogan "Making Disciples for the Transformation of the World." You ask, Is there no limit to contemporary Methodism's conceit and self-deceit? Not much. Thus is Jason's book a cheerful but clinch-fisted protest against about 90 percent of Methodist sermons that I hear and too many that I preach. In a church that's being decimated by overly earnest me-love-Bible-more-than-thou "traditionalists" and trendier-than-thou "progressives" (both groups hell bent on auto-salvation) Jason calls us to worship the odd sort of God who would die for sinners, only sinners.

Paul attempts to help the first Christians in Galatia deal with the shock that God really is in Christ doing for sinners—some whose sin is in their goodness—what they can't do for themselves. Jason thinks that the best thing the church can do for the world is exuberantly to announce who God actually is and what God is up to in the world: God is in Christ reconciling the world to God. And the best thing that the world can do is to relinquish their attachment to "religion" for the freedom of allowing ourselves to be loved by the God who, though we didn't know how to love, died for us anyway.

No preacher or pastor can read Jason's quite wonderful Galatians-inspired theological frolic without being encouraged (or shoved) to talk about the God who is for us rather than the godlet who is a divine personal trainer. Any of the baptized who read this book will be theologically rejuvenated by Jason's reminder of the adventure of life with so interesting a savior. And anybody who doesn't know much about the faith will be startled that Jesus is even odder than they thought.

After reading Jason's book, I announced to my fellow Methodists: you have messed up in so many ways and have squandered your *sola fide* inheritance for Mother-I'd-Rather-Save-Myself sermons. But one thing you did right. You didn't hinder God from producing one wildly entertaining, faithful preacher who really gets the outrageousness of the gospel and is bold enough to tell us all about it.

A Quid without Any Quo

Galatians 1:1–5

P AUL'S LETTER TO THE Galatians is at the very heart of the Protestant
Reformation's recovery of the doctrine of justification by grace alone in
Christ alone through faith alone according to Scripture alone. By many accounts the Epistle to the Galatians was the catalyst for the Great Awakening
in the eighteenth century, a movement of spiritual revival when hundreds
of thousands of men and women on both sides of the Atlantic heard the
gospel proclaimed clearly for the first time and, through the preaching of
the gospel, met the LORD Jesus Christ and were converted to a living faith
in him. For example, William Holland, a Methodist preacher who had recently returned from the American colonies to London, records in his diary
that on May 17, 1738, he was "providentially directed to Martin Luther's
Lectures on the Epistle to Galatians."

Holland writes in his diary:

> I carried the book round to Mr. Charles Wesley, who was sick at
> Mr. Bray's house, as though it were a very precious treasure that
> I had found, and we three sat down together. Mr. Charles Wes-
> ley read aloud Martin Luther's Preface to Galatians [Wherein
> Luther endeavors to explain the main argument and intention of
> St. Paul's Epistle as the necessary distinction between the law and
> the Gospel and "the more excellent righteousness of faith; that
> is, God through Christ, apart from any work of our own, cred-
> its righteousness freely to our account."] Mr. Wesley read these
> words of Luther, "What, have we then nothing—no works of the
> law to perform, no good deeds to do, no commands to obey—to
> do? Don't we have to work at all to obtain this righteousness? My
> answer is simple: Absolutely not, for this is perfect righteousness:
> To do nothing, to hear nothing, to know nothing about the law
> or works but only accept Him whom God has made for us all our
> wisdom and righteousness and sanctification and redemption." At

the words, "What, have we then nothing to do? No, nothing! but only accept Him . . . there came such a power over me as I cannot well describe; my great burden fell off in an instant; my heart was so filled with peace and love that I burst into tears. I almost thought I saw our Savior before me. My companions, perceiving me so affected, fell on their knees and prayed. Afterwards, when I went into the street, I could scarcely feel the ground I trod upon.[1]

Luther's short distillation of Paul's Letter to the Galatians and it's message of the gospel of grace so overwhelmed and astounded William Holland—who was a preacher, mind you—that afterwards, every day, he took the *Preface to Galatians* to the houses of friends and, knocking on their doors, would say, "Here, I have a promise so wonderful I'm desperate to share it with you. Can I tell you?"[2]

I've heard news so good I can't wait for you to hear it too.

He was a preacher, yet he was astonished by Paul's message in Galatians.

In other words, it's possible to be a preacher of the gospel and be preaching something other than the gospel.

Dorothy Sayers, the twentieth-century British novelist, was also a passionate and articulate Christian. In a justly famous op-ed for the *London Sunday Times*, she lamented how the Christian message is the most exciting drama that ever staggered the imagination of man, yet somehow preachers have pulled off the near-impossible feat of making the gospel boring. We make it sentimental: *God loves you just the way you are.* We make it moralistic: *Do unto others as you would have done to you.* We make it legalistic: *As a faithful follower of Christ, you must __________. Or, A faithful Christian ought not__________.* None of this requires Christ and his shed blood in order to be a coherent message. "We are constantly assured," Sayers complains, "that the churches are empty because preachers insist too much upon doctrine—'dull dogma,' as people call it. The fact is the precise opposite. It is the neglect of dogma that makes for dullness. The doctrine is the drama."[3] In other words, it's possible to be a community of the gospel—celebrating baptisms and consecrating bread and wine, singing hymns and studying the Bible, preaching and praying and serving the poor—that has lost the gospel. According to Sayers, a lack of eventfulness, excitement, expectation, surprise, playfulness, and astonishment—in other words,

---

1. Stott, *Message of Galatians*, 97.
2. Stott, *Message of Galatians*, 97.
3. Sayers, *Creed or Chaos?*, 80.

drama—are the telltale signs. It's possible to be a community created by the gospel that is no longer centered in the gospel. In his own journal, Charles Wesley also writes of the experience he shared with William Holland reading the *Preface to Galatians*:

> I marveled that we were so soon and entirely removed from him that called us into the grace of Christ and had fallen into another Gospel altogether. Who would believe from our preaching and teaching, or from the joy and freedom of our lives, that our Church had been founded upon this important article of justification by grace alone through faith alone? I am astonished and reproached by how this strikes me as a new doctrine.
>
> From this time forward I endeavored to ground as many of our friends as came in this fundamental truth, salvation by grace alone through faith alone.[4]

I've heard news so good I can't wait for you to hear it too.

One of those friends with whom Charles Wesley felt compelled to share the good news of justification by grace alone was his brother John, who, hearing the same distillation of the gospel a few days later at the Moravian chapel at Aldersgate in London, said that he felt his heart strangely warmed. John Wesley had been an ordained priest in the Church of England for ten years before it lit him on fire that all we need to do for our enoughness before God is "accept Him whom God has made for us all our righteousness."[5] Through John and Charles Wesley, the Holy Spirit unleashed a movement that fanned into flames thousands upon thousands, many of which, mind you, already identified as Christians. They were baptized. They were praying, good-deed-doing members of churches, and yet they responded to the gospel as though they were hearing it for the very first time, because they were hearing it for the very first time. In other words, it's possible to be a believer and be believing something other than the gospel.

Having a church is no guarantee of hearing the gospel.

Here's the rub: nobody ever drifts towards the gospel.

If you can remember those six words, then you're on your way to grasping Paul's argument with the Galatians: nobody ever drifts towards the gospel. Our inertia always will pull us away from the gospel, because the gospel does not come naturally to any of us. This is because the gospel comes as Jesus Christ and him crucified, which the Bible says is foolishness

---

4. Stott, *Message of Galatians*, 97.

5. Stott, *Message of Galatians*, 97.

to secular people, and a stumbling block even, perhaps especially, to religious people. Notice, for example, what's absent from Paul's short summary of the gospel: "The LORD Jesus Christ gave himself for our sins to set us free from the present evil age" (Gal 1:4–5). What's missing? You and I are denied a role as active agents. There is no mention of us contributing anything but sin to our salvation. The gospel is God's grace in Jesus Christ, not in partnership with us but in spite of us. Nor is there any mention of merit. The "our" in "who gave himself for our sins" is all-inclusive. God's grace omits no sinner. Christ is the incongruous gift of God given without any regard to the worth, gumption, piety, or stick-to-it-iveness of its recipients. For those of us who like to think we're worthy or maybe think we can become worthy with a little bit of help from God, the gospel is insulting. For those of us who know others who are worse than unworthy, the gospel is offensive. In a meritocracy like ours, the gospel is countercultural. In a just society like ours, the gospel risks sounding reckless and cheap. In a transactional world like ours, the gospel is counterintuitive. In Jesus Christ you have a quid without any demand for a quo.

As Robert Farrar Capon says, the gospel does not declare that God is like an Almighty Mother-in-law who gifts you a priceless crystal vase, but then every time she visits you she inspects it for nicks and scratches.[6] But the gravitational pull upon us from our transactional world will always be away from this gospel that gives us a quid without any demand for a quo. We simply can't drift toward the gospel; therefore, where the gospel is assumed, it's safe to assume the gospel has been lost. Even worse, where the gospel has been added to, the gospel has been annulled. When you make the gospel a stepping stone to something else, you're walking away from the gospel. And this is exactly what had happened in Galatia.

Dispatched by the Risen Christ, the apostle Paul had gone to Galatia, where he proclaimed the gospel and, through the power of the gospel, the grace of God had set people's hearts on fire. I have a promise so wonderful I'm desperate to share it with you. But as soon as Paul moved on to plant other churches beyond Galatia, false teachers from Jerusalem followed behind Paul. They claimed apostolic authority for themselves and taught a different gospel. "No," the false teachers preached, "contrary to what Paul told you, faith in the gospel alone is not sufficient to justify and save a sinner. You can't just enjoy your forgiveness. One day, God's going to judge you based on what you've done with your forgiveness. Sure, God's done his part, wiping

---

6. Capon, *Supper of the Lamb*, 12.

your slate clean in Jesus Christ, but now you've got to do your part, stomping out the sin in your life, standing up to sin in the world, and faithfully following his commands. There's got to be a quo for your quid."

The false teachers—Paul calls them Judaizers—were legalists, moralists. They muddled the message of the gospel with the law into a kind of glawspel. But glawspel, Paul writes in verse 7, is no gospel at all. There is no middle ground at all between: "Christ has done everything for you," and "This is what you must do." There is no reconciliation at all between those two messages. Paul's proposition is an all-or-nothing affair. In the grace of God in Jesus Christ and nothing else you have everything; therefore, Christ plus anything is nothing at all. The Gospel damns any and all additives to it, Martin Luther taught. "Now, if someone were so foolish as to presume to be made righteous, free, saved, and Christian through any good work," Luther writes in *The Freedom of a Christian*, "then such one would immediately lose faith along with all other good things."[7]

This is why the tone of Paul's letter to the churches in Galatia is so unlike his other epistles. Notice the very first word in the epistle, after Paul gives us his name and title, is NO: "Paul, an apostle—sent neither by human commission nor by human authorities . . ." Paul's first word for the Galatians is a no, and he's not even taking a second breath before he's calling for the wrath and judgment of God to fall upon their heads. Paul's Letter to the Galatians is proof that Paul would own everyone on social media. The epistle is angry and argumentative. It's polemical from beginning to end, drawing sharp contrasts and opposing antitheses. Paul is so alarmed by what he's heard of the churches in Galatia, like a mohel at a bris, he cuts the traditional thanksgiving from his salutation. In Corinth, church members had sex with their mothers-in-law, showed up drunk to the LORD's Table, and treated the poor like second-class citizens. Corinth is like the *Jersey Shore* of the New Testament, yet in his letters to them, Paul calls them saints and dear ones and he thanks God for them. But for the Galatians, Paul just writes, "To the churches of Galatia." And it goes downhill from there. Incidentally, this is another indication that Christianity is not a religion of morality; Christianity is the announcement of a message. If Christianity were about morality, then the Corinthians would be the last Christians whom Paul would call saints. If Christianity were about ethics, Paul would not launch his most heated verbal assault on the Galatians whose only

7. Luther, *Freedom of a Christian*, 43.

offense is muddling the message of the gospel. Rather than simply trusting the gospel, the Galatians were attempting to be good.

And they're the ones—not the Corinthians—upon whom Paul unleashes all his rhetorical fire.

Take note too that Paul addresses the letter to more than one church. He's writing to all the churches he and Barnabas had planted in the region of Galatia. He doesn't single any of them out for praise nor does he isolate the ones who deserve a friendly editor for their theology. He lumps them all together. Paul takes it for granted that everyone finds the false teachers' quid pro quo gospel, their Trusting Jesus + X message, attractive. He takes it for granted that they all find this false gospel alluring. And that should be a warning to us.

Five years ago my congregation did a sermon series on Galatians, and this letter once again prompted me to ask a friend in my congregation for a favor. I asked him to sit through an entire service one Sunday and do nothing but count the words we used in worship. I asked him to count all the gospel language we used in worship versus all the language of the law. From the announcements to the sermon, the prayers and songs and benediction, I asked him to pay attention and count how many words of comfort and promise we used compared to how many words of obligation and duty, ought and should.

"Done for you" versus "This you must do for God."

When he came up to me in the narthex after worship that Sunday, Mark pulled a moleskin notebook from his breast pocket and said, "I might've missed a few but it came out to about 85 percent to 15 percent."

"That's better than three-quarters," I replied, feeling prouder than proper. "That's better than I feared. That's pretty good."

"No," he said, "The other way around. "It was about 85 percent oughts and shoulds."

I grabbed his notebook and looked at his list of words. "Really?! You've got to be kidding me. Only 15 percent of our speech was Gospel?! I don't know what to do about 85 percent, or even know where to begin."

"Repent and beg God for forgiveness," he replied.

I looked up from Mark's notebook to see that he wasn't joking.

Nobody ever drifts towards the gospel. This is why in his salutation the apostle Paul does not refer to God as the maker of heaven and Earth or the LORD of Israel or the Father of Abraham, but immediately Paul refers to God as the Father of Christ Jesus who raised him from the dead. From the very first sentence of his letter, Paul points the Galatians to the resurrection because, as Paul writes, "Christ was handed over to death for our trespasses and was raised for our justification" (Rom 4:25). As Luther writes in his commentary, "Paul has nothing in his heart but the righteousness of Christ"[8] because the empty tomb is the passageway whereby Christ's very own righteousness becomes ours, free of charge, through faith. From the get-go, with nearly every iota and omicron of his letter, Paul is calling them back to the promise so wonderful he's still desperate to share it with them. And so am I, desperate as I am to share it. Because not only must we never assume the gospel as a church, we must always assume there's someone present in the church on the street or in the car seat next to you who desperately needs to hear the gospel. And their need to hear the gospel will always trump whatever else we might like to talk about on any given Sunday, whether it's politics, advice, life lessons, inspirational stories, or some other self-justifying activity. We can never assume the gospel or add to it, because we must always assume there's someone here, hanging on for dear life, who needs to hear the gospel and nothing but the gospel.

The doctrine is the drama.

One late Sunday afternoon I received an email from "Greg" who had visited us in worship that morning and stayed after for the Memorial Day service as well. He wrote:

> Dear Pastor,
>
> It was great to be back in church today. It's been too long. I stayed behind for the Memorial Day recognition and listened to your "bonus sermon." At least from my experience, I think you were spot on. I have been "a good Christian" my entire life. I've gone to service and given to the church and served the needy and kept the commandments. But in my work, on behalf of the nation, I cannot avoid the reality that I have personally and directly contributed to the death of hundreds if not thousands of people—people that my government, rightly or wrongly, viewed as evil. Even if they were evil, they're all still individuals for whom Christ died. I'm retired from the military now, but I still go to work every day and I labor to make our military more efficient and lethal in destroying other people. Thou shalt not kill? I pray constantly, pastor, that when I meet my Maker, he doesn't turn his face from me for what I have done and what I continue to do. I was willing to sacrifice my life

---

8. Luther, *Luther's Works*, 24:26.

for my nation's will, and I suppose I still am willing; nevertheless,
I now live with the burden of guilt of what I did and what I do.

Nobody ever drifts towards the gospel. We can never assume the gospel by skipping the step of announcing the good news, because we must always assume there's someone here who needs to hear it. Of course, the truth is we all need to hear it. Because the gospel is seemingly too good to be true, we never advance beyond needing to hear it, Sunday after Sunday. Greg certainly needs to hear it. So Greg, if you're reading, I have a promise so wonderful I'm desperate to share it with you, a promise I too depend upon like a frantic, drowning man clinging to a life preserver. The promise is that in Christ and him crucified you have been delivered into a new age, not of works but of grace. On account of Christ, everything that belongs to you—your sin—is his now. In Christ, everything that belongs to him—his righteousness, his perfect, permanent record—is yours now. Henceforth, for Christ's sake, God will never deal with you on the basis of your goodness or your badness but only the basis of Christ's finished work.

There are no pearly gates, and St. Peter's off doing something else, because his job as heavenly locksmith has been eliminated and the only record God will ever examine is Christ's. God will never deal with you on the basis of your goodness or your badness but only on the basis of Christ's finished work. And Greg, I've been a preacher of this promise long enough to know that, eventually, you're going to wonder: "But . . . but isn't there something I have to do?" The answer, Greg, is simple, and we have to hold fast to it because the gospel itself is at stake. The answer is, "No!" Absolutely not, for this is perfect righteousness: to do nothing, to hear nothing, to know nothing about the law or works but only accept him whom God has made for us all our wisdom and righteousness.

God-Damned Preachers

Galatians 1:6–10

I N HIS BOOK ON preaching, *Between Two Worlds*, the famed Anglican pastor-theologian John Stott recalls his ill-fated attempt to evangelize a classmate while they were both undergraduate students at Trinity College, Cambridge. Stott writes,

> Only recently had I come to Christ myself, and now—clumsily, I am sure—I was trying to share the good news with a fellow student. I was endeavoring to explain the great doctrine of justification by grace alone, that salvation was Christ's free gift, and that we could neither buy it nor even contribute to its purchase, for Christ had obtained it for us and was now offering it to us gratis. Suddenly, to my intense astonishment, my friend shouted at me three times at the top of his voice, "Horrible! Horrible! Horrible!" Such is the arrogance of the human heart that it finds the good news not glorious (which it is) but horrible (which it is not).[1]

In the decades that followed Christ's resurrection and ascension, there was a Jewish-Christian faction within the fledgling church, called the Judaizers, who insisted that Paul's gospel was horrible. Paul's gospel was a gospel of free grace for sinners. As Paul testifies before the Ephesian elders in the book of Acts, "I do not count my life of any value to myself, if only I may finish my course and the ministry that I received from the LORD Jesus, to testify to the good news of God's grace" (Acts 20:24). Paul's gospel was a gospel of justification whereby, on account of Christ's cross and resurrection, our performance file in the Almighty's heavenly HR department contains nothing but Christ's perfect, permanent record. Or, as Paul summarizes his gospel message for the Corinthians, "For our sake God made him to be sin who knew no sin, so that in him we might become the righteousness of God" (2 Cor 5:21).

1. Stott, *Between Two Worlds*, 242.

Horrible. Horrible. Horrible.

The Judaizers found the apostle Paul's gospel offensive. After all, if salvation is for sinners, then salvation is for everyone. But if salvation is free for everyone, then those of us who are good get demoted to the same rank as the ungodly, and whatever righteousness I have earned through my works and obedience no longer has any value at all. It's like currency left over in my wallet from a trip I took to a foreign country—a foreign country whose government has since collapsed. Therefore, when Paul ventured into Asia Minor, the Judaizers followed close behind him and attempted to persuade the churches Paul had planted that his gospel was wrong. That his gospel was incomplete. That it was horrible. And as we see in the Epistle to the Galatians, to Paul's "astonishment," the false teachers faced little opposition as they perverted the gospel message of grace and led the churches in Galatia astray. The false teachers' approach was an easy commodity to market, because it removed the offense of the gospel and restored to it the easy accounting and the comfort of merit and demerit.

You can see their message plainly in the book of Acts where the gospel writer Luke reports that they taught the Christians in Antioch that "Unless you are circumcised according to the custom of Moses, you cannot be saved" (Acts 15:21). Realize circumcision was not merely a religious ritual, and it was more than a sign of membership in the people of God. Circumcision was the entrypoint to a life of obedience under the law. In other words, the false teachers were not imploring the Galatians to undergo an isolated, arbitrary, antiquated operation; they were insisting the Galatians undertake all the obligations of the law (in both the Old Testament and in the earthly teaching of Christ). The success of the false teachers' rival message owed to its subtlety. They did not deny that you must rely upon Jesus Christ for your salvation, but they implied it wasn't enough. They instead preached that you must reply upon Jesus Christ and the law for your salvation. You must turn back to Moses, the false teachers taught, to finish what Christ began. God's done his part, wiping your slate clean in Jesus Christ, but now you've got to do your part: stomp out the sin in your life, stand up to sin in the world, and faithfully follow his commands.

The false teachers did not deny the gospel. They muddled it with the law. A mixture that turned it into a different message entirely, glawspel. We're all bookkeepers at heart, Paul writes in Romans. And what makes the gospel offensive is not what it demands from us but what it gives to us freely, to all of us, without regard to worth. *Free forgiveness?! For him?! But he drank away his life savings and walked out on his wife and three kids with nary a regret! Christ's own righteousness?! For them?! But they're so racist they've done everything but burn a cross in their neighbor's yard.*

Horrible. Horrible. Horrible.

Sure, we all fall short of the glory of God, but if there are good works we must do, we need to throttle sin as our necessary response to the gospel—if there's something we must do, then at least some of us can inch closer to glory, climb higher in holiness, and score better than others. We all desperately want our Heavenly Father to sport a bumper sticker on his celestial Lexus that says, "My child is an Honor Roll Student at the School of the Life." We don't want a gospel where God says to us, "Well done, good and faithful servant," on the basis of Christ's work alone. Faith + Something of Our Own always appeals to our inner accountant. But glawspel is no gospel at all, the apostle Paul writes to the Galatians. And actually the word Paul uses in verse 7, *metastrepho*, means "to turn inside out." In other words, when we alter the gospel in any way we not only annul the gospel, we pervert it into its opposite. This is what Paul, in his Letter to the Corinthians, calls "a ministry of death" (2 Cor 3:7). "Even if a cute, chubby cherub angel with ivory wings and golden fleece diapers showed up on the *Rachel Maddow Show* proclaiming to you a gospel contrary to the one given to us by the Risen Christ, then let that one be anathema!" Paul hollers in the Jason Micheli paraphrase edition of the Bible.

Anathema. Accursed.

It's worse than horrible.

Anathema.

Literally, it means "God-damned."

In August 1960, not long before he graced the cover of *Time Magazine*, the renowned Swiss theologian Karl Barth met the still-more-famous American preacher Billy Graham while they both vacationed in the Valais region of Switzerland. According to letters Barth wrote to friends, their meeting was a friendly one. "He's a jolly good fellow," Barth wrote of Graham, "with whom one can talk easily and openly; one has the impression that he is even capable of listening, which is not always the case with such trumpeters of the Gospel."[2] Two weeks later, Barth had the same good impression of Billy Graham after they met for a second time at Barth's home in Basel. It was during that second visit that Graham invited Barth to be a guest at the revival he would be preaching that night in the city. Over

---

2. Busch, *Karl Barth*, 446.

15,000 showed up at the St. Jacob Stadium in downtown Basel. Hearing Graham preach his message and witnessing his influence over the mass of young people, Karl Barth was not impressed. He was outraged.

Anathema.

"I was quite horrified," Barth wrote to his son, "Graham acted like a madman, and what he presented was certainly not the Gospel. It was the Gospel with a gun. It was the Gospel with a threat attached. An urgent appeal was made to the people: You must do this! You should not do that! It was a proclamation of the law not the message of the Gospel. He attempted to terrify people into the Gospel. Threats, they always make an impression."[3]

Imperatives—this you must do—make sense to us. But even this preacher's success and the size of his crowds and the breadth of his fame do not justify such preaching. The messenger and his success do not validate the message. The message validates the messenger. It is illegitimate to pervert the gospel into law. We must leave God the freedom to do all the work. When the good news of the grace of God in Jesus Christ comes with anything else attached it is no longer the gospel. It is a different gospel altogether, which is no gospel at all. A few years later, during his first and only visit to the United States, at a press conference at the University of Chicago, reporters asked Karl Barth to elaborate on his exasperation with the rival preacher's message and method. Christian faith begins with joy, not with fear because the gospel is that there is nothing we must do because everything has already been done for us. "Mr. Graham," Barth said to the press, "he begins by making people afraid."[4]

Anathema.

The good news of the gospel is that you can rest in the work of Christ Jesus.

Faith does nothing but grasp ahold of what Christ has already done for you. There is now no sin other than forgiven sin. And there is now no work that is necessary for you to do for anyone other than for your neighbor. The good news of the gospel is that you can rest in the work of Christ. Anything else, anything extra, anything added, is anathema.

When I was an undergraduate at the University of Virginia, I applied and interviewed to be a leader for Young Life's campus ministry. During my face-to-face interview, the assistant to the regional manager (or whatever his title was) indicated his expectation that, included with any

---

3. Busch, *Karl Barth*, 449.

4. Busch, *Karl Barth*, 449.

presentation of the gospel I offered to them, I would steer students away from drugs, drunkenness, and casual sex. He wanted me to preach faith in Christ's work + some work of their own. And because I was a relatively new Christian, I hadn't had much time to drift away from the gospel, so I didn't know any better. Attempting to sound decisive whilst sitting enveloped in an overstuffed sofa, I said: "But that's not the gospel. No doubt, everyone would be better off if students stayed away from drugs, drank a little less, and kept it in their pants, but their failure to do so does not undo the truth of the gospel. They can have a joint on their lips, empties all around their feet, and a girl whose name they don't remember in the morning . . . and it still doesn't change the gospel." He made notes in the margins of my application as I spoke.

Horrible. Horrible. Horrible.

Because I was a relatively new Christian, I was surprised—astonished—to discover, a week later, that my application had been rejected.

Once you understand the offense of the gospel and the attraction of the law, you realize that, as the church, we are always on the precipice of the Galatian heresy. We're forever tempted to rip the pillow out from underneath sinners' heads, to give them something they must do, to prevent them from resting in Christ and his righteousness alone.

So here's how you spot a false gospel:

- If it makes you anxious or afraid, it's another gospel.

- If it leaves you feeling exhausted or burned out or guilty, it's some other gospel.

- If it insists that in order to be a good Christian you must belong to this political party, you must not support that candidate, you should have this interpretation of Scripture for that issue, and/or you ought to abstain from these critical theories, it's a different gospel.

- If it's about your behavior rather than Christ's, if it's about your need to believe in anything other than his saving work for you, it's not the gospel.

And—I say this for all the mainline preachers eavesdropping—if what you are preaching can be true without requiring the shed blood of Jesus Christ for sinners, it's no gospel at all. The message has been turned inside out. St. Paul today summons a solemn, fearful anathema for all those who dare to alter the gospel. Notice Paul issues the anathema twice. This is more than hyperbole or rhetorical passion. In the Greek Old Testament, it's the same word for the divine curse that God executes at the fall. Paul's praying for there to be pillars of salt in every pulpit where anything but the gospel is proclaimed. So I got it wrong this Sunday, there's always next Sunday, right? Why does Paul make getting the gospel right a matter of four-letter fire and brimstone? Look, the answer is in verse 6. Paul uses the language of betrayal. Notice Paul doesn't say that in turning to a different gospel they've turned traitor to Paul. Paul doesn't accuse them of betraying the other apostles or the church. Paul writes that they have spurned "the one who called you in the grace of Christ."

The one who called you. The verb in Greek is *kaleo*. Here's the thing: Paul never uses the verb *kaleo* with himself or any other person as the one calling. Throughout all of Scripture, "the one who calls" (*ho kalon*), functions as a name for God. Paul is filled with four-letter fury over the Galatians being led astray from the gospel because God himself gives himself to you in the gospel. *Ex nihilo*, the Living Word verbs you into existence as a new creation in the gospel announcement. The reason the gospel alone has the power to change you is that the gospel is a promise that gives you Christ himself; and with him, everything that belongs to him—all of his righteousness, all of his faithfulness, all of his forgiveness and mercy. The gospel is first-order discourse, not second-order discourse. First-order discourse is a mode of address that changes the relationship between speaker and person; e.g., "I love you" or "F*ck you!" Second-order discourse is mere description ("God is love") and changes nothing. To turn to a different gospel isn't merely to turn to a different message; it's to lay the Maker of all that is back down in his Bethlehem manger and walk away.

One afternoon at my church, a few months before the Coronavirus pandemic, a young woman wandered into the church. The hijab wrapped loosely around her head was as brightly colored as her MacBook was covered in stickers. "I'm looking for a preacher," she said.

I greeted her as the pastor, and she introduced herself as a student at George Mason University.

"I'm enrolled in a class on Comparative Religions," she explained, "and as part of our final paper, we're supposed to interview religious leaders about how their communities worship and why."

Her name was Adeela. Because she'd wandered in through the narthex, I showed Adeela around the sanctuary. I told her how the first Christians built their sanctuaries in the shape of a cross and oriented them to face east, the direction of the rising sun. I showed her my robe and explained how the color black symbolized sin, and I added how, in John Wesley's day, preachers would wear a white surplice overtop the black cassock as a visual reminder of baptism clothing us in Christ's righteousness. I showed her the lectern, and the pulpit.

"From the one, we read the word of God. From the other, we hear the word of God."

"How do you decide what Scripture to preach?" she asked me.

"Well, the text determines the sermon," I said, "but we believe every passage points us to Christ, to the gospel. So, in theory, every sermon should be a variation on the same theme."

She looked at me funny, not following.

"For instance," I said, "this coming Sunday—it's the parable of the prodigal son, from Luke's Gospel."

I saw her sounding out the word prodigal like she'd never heard it before. So I summarized the story Jesus tells about the father who had two sons, the youngest of whom one day wished his father dead, demanded his share of the inheritance, forsook his family's home, and departed for a different life in a far country. Only after the spoiled, rotten kid wasted his last dime and found himself panhandling along the median on the highway—only then did the prodigal son decide to press his luck by returning to his father's house.

"What happened when he came home?" Adeela asked with an interest that, to be honest, I am unaccustomed to.

"As soon as he appeared on the horizon, his father ran out to embrace him," I said, "The whole time he was gone his father had been rocking the front porch rocker, waiting for his return."

"And then what happened?" Adeela asked, her voice on the edge of its seat.

"Well, then, the father wrapped the prodigal son in his own robe, gave him the family ring off his finger, and ordered the foreman of the ranch to kill the fatted calf because they had got no excuse not to throw a party."

"But wait," Adeela said, "Hold up. Didn't the son apologize? Make amends? Do something to restore his father's honor?"

"No," I replied, "No, the father forgave him without an ounce of repenting."

"But surely his father punished him in some way, right?"

"No."

"Alright, but tell me he pays back the inheritance he squandered."

"Nope."

She looked at me with something shy of contempt. "Well, does he at least learn his lesson? Change? Become a different person?"

"Jesus never says," I told her. "The story's about the father's forgiveness and love, not the son's sin and repentance."

"I think Jesus should've at least mentioned it," she said, shaking her head.

"That's what all religious people think," I replied. "But if you add anything else to the story—the prodigal cleaning up his act, say, or the father warning him there'll be no next-time second chances—if you add anything to the story, you've irreparably changed the story."

"You said every story in the Bible points to Jesus. Where's he in the story, then?"

"Oh, that's easy," I said. "Jesus is the fatted calf whose sole purpose is to die in order for the spendthrift father to throw a party for his undeserving son."

I could read it on her face: Horrible, horrible, horrible.

"If that's true," she said, "then that's why I could never be a Christian."

And sure, I wasn't trying to evangelize her exactly, but notice she said no to the gospel because of the gospel's offensiveness. That is, she said no to Christianity for the right reason. She didn't say no to Christianity because Christians are partisan. She didn't say no to Christianity because Christians are hypocritical. She didn't say no to Christianity because Christians are judgmental. She didn't say no to Christianity for the wrong reasons. She said no for the right reason. She said no because the gospel is offensive. I showed her around the church a bit more, answering her questions and asking her about her studies. Just before she left to catch a bus, she turned around and looked at me, the sanctuary door half-open.

"A lot of my classmates think all religions are basically the same," she said, "but if what you said about that story is true, then they're wrong. Your message is completely different, and it's why I could never be a Christian."

And then she walked away.

May God have mercy on me—we're all in this together, so may God have mercy on you too, dear reader—if we ever add anything to our message in order to win over someone like her.

Apocalypto

Galatians 1:11–24

I N HIS MEMOIR, *ACCIDENTAL Preacher*, Duke Divinity School Professor Bishop Will Willimon testifies to being encountered one late afternoon in 1975. Having locked up the doors of Trinity United Methodist church in Myrtle Beach, South Carolina, Will was walking across the churchyard to the tiny parsonage for supper.

> My heart sank when I turned and saw a young man, late twenties, perhaps early thirties, coming down the church walk. Just my rotten luck. These drifters passed through North Myrtle Beach. Their hard luck stories differed, but all had the same ending, "Give me twenty-five dollars." I'll head him off, give him a twenty, and be rid of him. Don't have it in me, this late in the day, to hear any more trumped-up tales of woe. "Hello!" he called to me cheerfully. "Hello." "You're working late this afternoon, aren't you?" 'What can I do for you?" "Not a thing, other than what you are already doing," he said. "Good work." Odd comment.
>
> "I just stopped by to tell you I think you are doing a great job here at Trinity." "Is it Miami or Charleston that you need money to get to?" I asked with annoyance. "Money? No," he laughed. 'I just stopped by to tell you that I appreciate all you do to get the good news out to folks. Nice work. Your sermons rock." I looked at him more carefully. He had a dark tan and was wearing khakis, scuffed loafers, and a green golf shirt. Izod. He didn't look crazy, though in this town, it can be hard to tell. I saw no hint of a weapon. "Say," he continued, "do you get much time to read the Bible?" "Er, uh, sure. I read Scripture every day," I answered. So this is his shtick. He's going to wear me down with chitchat before making the ask.
>
> "What do you think of it?" he asked. "Uh, the Bible? I like it. I think it's good," I said. "Thanks! 'Course, I had some great folks working with me. Glad to see it's still in print! Right?" he said jovially, buddy-tapping me lightly on the arm. "Right," I said, my

throat tightening. I assessed him closely. He looked like he had just walked off the Gator Hole Golf Course. "Let me guess what your favorite gospel is. Luke! Am I right? I bet you like Luke as a writer, don't you?" he said. "What a cool job Luke did on the parables. Right?" As if the busted fall stewardship campaign was not humiliating enough, now this. "Hey, just wanted to stop by and thank you. I'm sure it's not easy in this town. Really appreciate your hard work. You're a go-getter. Pay no mind to the trustees. I'll bring 'em around, eventually. The jail ministry you guys started last year is going just great," he said, moving toward me as if to threaten a hug. "Don't worry about the stewardship thing. The money will come, I'm sure," he said patronizingly. I took a step back. "Sorry, I didn't get your name." "Oh, that's funny," he said, laughing. "Just Jesus to you, of course." "Look, are you trying to be cute?" I asked. "You think that's cute?" he responded, looking hurt. "Hey, don't want to keep you from the valuable work you are doing. But please, don't overdo it. Remember, Trinity is my problem, not yours. Help people, go ahead and preach, write, just be sure you have a good time."

"Uh, if you're Jesus, where are you headed?" I asked. "Akron, Ohio," he said casually. "Akron, Ohio?" I asked. "Business," he responded.

And as Will finishes his remembrance, he writes:

He took my hand, drawing me uncomfortably close, giving off a slight whiff of garlic and cigarettes, and said, "Well done, friend." I received his embrace as stiffly as if I were Richard Nixon being hugged by Sammy Davis Jr. Yet as I watched him head towards the highway where he hitched a ride from a green Toyota, I thanked God for my credulous childhood, and also for some proficiency in dealing with the comings and goings of a God both friendly and mischievous.[1]

I know what you're thinking. It's a weird, crazy story, right? I mean, Jesus wearing a green golf shirt and pleated dockers? Come on, Jesus would be rolling in his grave if he knew some headcase reeking of Marlboro Reds was stealing his identity along the boardwalk. There has to be a better explanation, right? Surely, this wayfaring stranger had to have been a burnt-out, delusional drifter, right? Nothing exposes our functional atheism quite like a story like Willimon's. Nothing reveals our functional atheism more than our reaction to claims of revelation. Look, I get it. I

1. Willimon, *Accidental Preacher*, 220.

empathize with your knee-jerk skepticism. I swim in the same water as you. On any given month, I've got thousands upon thousands of dollars of chemotherapy coursing through my blood. Trust me, I believe in science and logic and rational observation. But the trouble is that I, too, can testify to having been encountered.

It was homecoming morning in Charlottesville in 1999. A month into the fall semester of my fourth year at the University of Virginia, I'd planned to skip the football game and was holed up at an empty carrel back in the stacks of the old Alderman library. I had a Bible on the desk for a class I was taking on the Gospel of John. I also had a couple of LSAT prep books I'd already started to dog-ear and underline. At the library carrel on the other side of the row of bookcases was a tall, skinny, African American man wearing large headphones and an orange-and-navy track suit. He was busy highlighting a biochemistry textbook and taking notes on colored index cards. I'd started working on some sample problems from the prep book when suddenly there was a guy leaning against the end of the bookcase, with his feet crossed nonchalantly and a crinkly, plastic-covered book in his hands.

"What are you workin' on?"

"Me? Um, studying for the LSAT," I said.

He had a beard on a tan face and dark hair that stuck out from the black knit hat on his head. He was wearing jeans that were ripped at the knees and a brown Henley shirt.

"You've got a lot of lawyers in your family already, don't you?"

"Yes," I said. "Wait, how did you . . . ?"

"Don't freak out, Jason," he said, and pulled a different book—anthropology—from the shelf and flipped through it. "You like that other class a lot, don't you?" he said, pointing at the *Harper Collins Study Bible*.

"Yeah, I really do," I said. "But I like the other classes too. It's hard, you know, knowing what God wants you to do with your life."

"I just want you to enjoy your life," he said.

I looked around for my roommates who surely must be punking me.

"Don't do anything just to satisfy someone else's expectations and don't go down any path just to measure up to what the world defines as success. That's what I freed you from," he said, smiling. And then he pointed at the Bible and said, "If you'll have the most fun doing that, then that's what you should do." He slid the book back in the empty space on the bookshelf. He held out his arm to fist bump me and said, "Relax, man. You're going to have a grand time."

"Hold up," I said, trying to find my voice, "I didn't catch your name."

But he'd already disappeared behind the graffitied, heavy fire door at the end of the long row of stacks. After a few moments, I turned to the premed student on the other end of the bookcase. Speaking up so as to be heard over his headphones, I said, "Did you catch that guy's name?"

"What guy? Nobody been here, boss, but you and me."

Not long after, when I started the process that led to ordination as a pastor, I learned not to tell that story. Clergy, ironically enough, were the quickest to think I was crazy and ask if I'd sought counseling.

Here at the beginning of his emotional appeal to the churches in Galatia, the apostle Paul has just laid down four-lettered fire and brimstone. "If anyone preaches to you a gospel other than the gospel I handed down to you," Paul writes with all-caps urgency, "if anyone adds a single ought or should to the gospel, let that one be anathema." The exclusivity of Paul's gospel begs the question: "Who died and made you the sole authority, Paul?"

"Why should we listen to Paul?" the false teachers whispered to the churches in Galatia. "Where did he get this gospel of his anyway? After all, Paul didn't even know Jesus."

Anticipating the false teachers' disqualifications, the apostle Paul testifies today that the gospel of grace is neither a human invention and nor is it a religious tradition. It is a revelation. "For I did not receive the gospel," Paul writes, "from another human being, nor was I taught it by a human being; it came to me by an apocalypse of Jesus Christ." The word most Bibles translate as "revelation" is the Greek word meaning "to uncover" or "to disclose" but also "to break in upon" and "to invade." The gospel I handed down to you, Paul is saying, I received in a manner no different than Peter or the other disciples—I received it directly from the LORD Jesus Christ, whom I did not know in his mortal life but who met me in the reality of his risen life.

In the book of Acts, Luke corroborates Paul's recollection to the Galatians. Saul, who'd already been an accessory to the murder of Stephen, was on his way to Damascus with arrest warrants when he was encountered by the Risen Jesus: "Saul, Saul, why do you persecute me?" (Acts 9:4).

Meanwhile, Luke adds, the Risen Christ was busy back in town, breaking in upon the life of a disciple named Ananias. "The LORD said to Ananias in a vision, 'Ananias. Get up and go and look for a man of Tarsus named Saul . . . lay hands on him . . . for he is an instrument whom I have chosen to preach my gospel before gentiles and kings and all the people of Israel" (Acts 9:10, 11, 12, 15).

The Risen Christ *apocalypsed* into Ananias's life too. Incidentally, this is why Paul refuses to let go of his gospel of grace apart from the law. Paul's experience is his own sermon illustration for the message Christ gave him to preach. What Paul thought was his merit according to the law turned out to be nothing more than innocent blood on his hands. In his zeal to perform works of righteousness for God, he had in fact been sinning against none other than the LORD himself. Paul refuses to back down from the gospel of grace, not only because it's what Jesus Christ taught him but also because Paul himself is exhibit A that in Jesus Christ God justifies the ungodly—God gives to sinners the righteousness his law demands. Perhaps nothing underscores Paul's message of unmerited grace, apart from any work of our own, more than God's prenatal call of Paul. That Paul can look back on his life with what C. S. Lewis calls "grace-colored glasses"[2] and conclude that God had set him apart in utero is good news for you in two ways. Firstly, no matter the circumstances of your life, no matter how acutely you perceive his absence or how many unanswered prayers you can count, God is always—God is never not—at work in your life. Secondly, there is nothing you can do—no sin you can commit, no obligation you can neglect, no calling you can ignore—to thwart the purposes and plans of God for your life. Saul was church Enemy Number One, but Paul becomes the church's chief apostle precisely because God had set him apart for that very task. You don't need to be a Sunday school graduate to know the story of Saul being blinded by the light on the way to Damascus. What most Christians don't realize, however, is that, the scales having fallen from his eyes, Paul did not immediately set out from Damascus preaching the gospel. As he writes to the Galatians today, Paul entered a self-imposed exile in Arabia where for three years he was tutored in the gospel by the Risen Christ. According to John Stott, "those three years in Arabia were a deliberate compensation for the three years of instruction which Jesus gave the other apostles, but which Paul missed."[3] The reason the apostle Paul was adamant that he was preach-

2. Stott, *Message of Galatians*, 71.

3. Stott, *Message of Galatians*, 82.

ing the true gospel, even though he suffered greatly for it, was that for three years he was taught this gospel by the one who is the truth that sets us free: "The gospel that was proclaimed by me is not of human origin; for I did not receive it from a human source, nor was I taught it, but I received it through an apocalypse of Jesus Christ" (Gal 1:11).

I get the knee-jerk skepticism. A three-year, one-on-one Bible study with a tutor who was tortured to death two years earlier? As I've said, I swim in the same water as you. I've got terminal cancer; my life literally depends on science. I believe in logic and rational observation, but how else do you explain that, years later, when Paul makes his way to Jerusalem, not only is Paul's Gospel recognized by the other apostles as the true gospel, but these same apostles accept the apostolic authority of Paul despite the fact that he had once hunted them down and stoned them? What can account for their acceptance of Paul and his Gospel? Paul had their blood on his hands.

But they knew that Jesus was not dead. And they knew this gospel preached by Paul sounded eerily similar to the gospel the Risen Christ had revealed to Peter in a dream. What could possibly have compelled them to submit to Paul's apostolic authority other than revelation?

A colleague in ministry told me the story of a friend named Nesteron, who lived in Iran, in a region where the gospel is neither known nor available. Nesteron belonged to an observant Muslim family, yet one day Jesus apocalypsed into her life and made himself known to her.

"What was it like?" my colleague asked her.

"It wasn't like an audible voice, but it wasn't like a voice in my head either. It was something altogether different but altogether real."

Unbeknownst to Nesteron, at this same time, her sister, who was studying in Europe, had received the gospel from a classmate and was baptized. Jesus later appeared to her and told her that she needed to go back home and share his gospel with Nesteron and their family. When Nesteron's sister arrived back at their family's home in Iran, Nesteron greeted her by saying, "I know—you're here to tell me about Jesus. I believe in him. I've met him."

A month later, Nesteron's father received a vision of Jesus in a dream. "Jesus spoke to me," he said, "He was dressed in a color like no color I have ever seen before."

I could tell you so many stories.

There's Diane, who was a member of my first congregation in New Jersey. The first funeral I ever preached was for Diane's father, who came home from work one afternoon, went down to the basement, and committed suicide. Before the police were able to reach Diane and break the news to her, Jesus came to her.

"He was standing in the kitchen, on the linoleum floor, in front of the microwave and toaster oven. I don't know how I knew it was him, because he didn't say anything, but I knew he wanted to comfort me for some reason. Jesus wanted to comfort me, and here I was embarrassed by all the dirty dishes in the sink."

There's Hector, who was an inmate at the prison where I served as chaplain. Hector came to see me one hot summer day, his olive skin blanched white from fright.

"Man, no joke, Jesus Christ was just there—in my cell—last night before lights out. He told me everything I done is all forgiven. And then he told me my kids are going to be alright. Preacher, don't you get it? Everyone up in here is trying to get out and Jesus Christ broke in to tell me I'm forgiven."

Hector looked terrified, but it didn't stop him from asking me to baptize him on Sunday.

God broke in, he said. *Apocalypsed.*

Look, I get it. Every bit as much as you, I have been conditioned by the Enlightenment's lack of imagination. Nevertheless! The way the Risen Jesus *apocalypsed* into Paul's life, it's different in degree but not in kind from the way Christ reveals himself to all of us. Indeed, this is Paul's whole point here in Galatians. It's not just that Paul received the gospel by revelation that one time on the road to Damascus; it's that reception of the gospel always comes only by revelation.

Paul's calling in grace is unique, yes, but it is not singular. Reception of the gospel always comes by no other means than revelation. Whether it's a preacher lofting the gospel into your ears or the gospel being handed to you in bread and wine, or the gospel promise sung to you in an anthem by a choir, whether you dreamed a dream or received a vision or were blinded by the light, reception of the gospel always comes by revelation. To the extent that you grasp the promise of the gospel, to the extent that you trust that all of your sins belong to Christ and all of his righteousness belongs to you, it's because you have been grasped by the gospel. No, it's because you have been grasped by God through his gospel. This is exactly what Jesus says at the feeding of the 5,000: "No one can come to me unless the Father who sent me draws them to me" (John 6:44). And Jesus says it again after the raising of Lazarus: "When I am lifted up from the earth, I will be drawing all people to myself" (John 12:32). Thomas Jefferson famously redacted the Bible, excising from the New Testament all those passages Jefferson deemed too supernatural for a rational, scientific child of the Enlightenment any longer to believe. But if Jefferson understood what Paul asserts about the nature of the gospel, Jefferson would have had no choice but to remove all of the apostle's letters as well. Because Paul is claiming that every time we proclaim the gospel we become conduits of the Jesus who is not dead. Every time we share the promise of the gospel, we become conduits by which the Risen Christ can reveal his grace to others. We are his apocalyptic means. It can appear as simple an act as you reassuring a friend with a troubled conscience that, on account of Christ, the entirety of their sins are forgiven—Paul's point is that that's an apocalyptic event. Those are the cracks where the Living God breaks in upon us. We marvel at or we puzzle over the mysterious, blinding-light type encounters with Jesus, but the sheer fact that any of us believe the gospel is every bit as miraculous and supernatural as loaves and fishes or walking on water or summoning forth the dead from their tombs. Whether it's as slight as a mustard seed or as massive as mountain, your faith is the crater left behind by the apocalypse of God.

A couple of summers ago, after reading a draft of Will Willimon's memoir, I asked him, "How is it that I've listened to all of your sermons several times over and read nearly every one of your books, yet I've never heard your story about being met by Jesus outside that church in Myrtle Beach?" Will chuckled and said:

> I quickly discovered that if I told anyone that story, especially in a sermon, then most people just wanted to ask me how they could have such an experience for themselves, as though the experience is somehow more important than the message. The message is more important than the experience—that's why, for example, Paul doesn't say much more than a sentence about his own encounter with the Risen Christ but he never tires of preaching the forgiveness of sins. Besides, if only God can reveal God, then I've got no advice on how you can have an experience of Christ. Anyone who claims they do is a liar, and any experience of God that can be choreographed is not the Living God. The only place we know to go

where we can expect to be met by Christ is the place Christ has promised to show up, and that's in the gospel.

And he does show up. Against the tide we are all swimming in, he shows up. I could tell you so many stories. A kid, a graduating senior, came up to me in the parking lot after the Baccalaureate service for the local high school. He'd already loosened his tie and unzipped his graduation gown. Squinting in the sun, he said to me, "You know, you're not much of a preacher. You talked too fast and you tried too hard to charm us. Still, I don't know how else to explain it but somehow God broke through your not very good sermon and, in spite of you, God spoke to me today."

"Are you just messing with me, kid?"

"No."

"Well, what do you think God said to you in my apparently inadequate sermon?"

"He said that it doesn't matter what I make of my education and opportunities because, in Jesus, I'm already enough and no failure or success can change that."

I took a step back from him, like I'd accidentally tip-toed onto holy ground.

"Do you think that sounds like something Jesus would say?" he asked.

"Kid, I know for a fact that it's something Jesus would say."

All You Need Is Nothing

Galatians 2:1–10

I T HAPPENS EVERY CHRISTMAS and Easter. Sometimes it happens on other Sundays, but it always happens every Christmas and Easter. And it's nothing particular about me. Every pastor I know can tell the same stories of the sorts of people who linger around after "Silent Night" has been sung or the resurrection "Alleluia" has been proclaimed, and then, as though they want to show the burn mark where the lightning struck, they approach the preacher to share how the good news hit them in the brokenness of their lives that day. A man approached me at the end of the seven o'clock Christmas Eve service, just before the pandemic. I was standing along the altar rail. Smoke was still rising from the wick of my candle. I felt the warm, soft wax on his fingers as I shook his hand and said, "Merry Christmas!"

He blushed and mumbled the season's greeting back to me, clearly second-guessing his impulse to come forward. He had salt-and-pepper hair and razor burn on cheeks that were deeply creased and made him look older than I guessed him to be. The hood of his red Patagonia parka was pulled up over his head—probably, I supposed, to hide the tears running down his face like water on a shower wall.

"I'm Jason," I said, "I'm one of the preachers here."

"I know," he said. "That would be quite the outfit if you weren't the preacher."

I laughed and then let the silence that followed fester, waiting for him to show me whatever glad wound God had left behind on him.

"Your message . . ." he said, the words catching in his throat, "your message tonight made me want to become a Christian."

I've learned to expect people like him on Christmas and Easter, but I hadn't expected him to say that.

"The message made you want to become a Christian? Well, what's stopping you? We can seal the deal right here and now."

He shook his head. Hard. As much as he wanted to become a Christian, he did *not* want to become a Christian.

"What's stopping me? I've got a dresser drawer full of thirty-day sobriety coins but not a single other one. I've got a wife who doesn't know I lost my job—I just drive all day and drink in my car. I've got a son who won't talk to me—for good reasons—and I've got a father whom I've never forgiven for walking out."

I didn't say anything. I waited for him to flesh out the problem.

"Do you see? Preacher, it's all I can do to get out of bed every day. It felt like walking on broken glass just to be here tonight. If I become a Christian, then I'll have to commit myself ,won't I? I'll have to commit to getting sober and telling the truth to my wife and patching things up with my son and my father. To be a Christian, I'll have to commit to doing those things and— I've already lived too many lies—the truth is, I know I can't do it all. Like I said, your message tonight . . . it made me want to be a Christian, but to be a Christian, I'll have to promise to do those other things too, won't I?"

And I looked at him, opened my mouth, and flubbed it. Like a gymnast who can't stick the landing, what I said to him completely undid whatever I'd said earlier that made him want to be a Christian. I said, "Well, maybe so, but you don't have to do it all tonight."

That wasn't a yes, exactly. Yes, in order to be a Christian you're compelled to get clean, confess to your missus, reconcile with your son, and forgive your father. I didn't say yes, exactly. I didn't fail that badly. But I did not give him the single-syllabled, solitary word that he desperately needed to hear and that just happens to be the God's-honest truth. I said a great many things to him. Pastoral things, perhaps. Compassionate things, probably. Empathetic things, I bet. But I know, from sheer word count, that I did not clearly and emphatically, with an urgency that made plain this is a matter of death and life on which the gospel itself is at stake, say "*No.*" No, you don't have to clean up your act in order to be a Christian. No, you don't have to confess and repent in order to be a Christian. No, you don't have to reconcile and forgive in order to be a Christian. *No!* You don't need to have any of that to your credit to be a Christian. In fact, all you need to have is nothing.

I know it because the Bible tells me so, like here in Galatians.

It's likely not your most beloved memory verse, and I doubt any of you have it cross-stitched and framed on your wall, but I could make a case that verse 3 in our text today is one of the most consequential, record-scratching, mic-dropping verses in the entire Bible: "Titus was not compelled to be circumcised." You might not want "Titus was not compelled to be circumcised" stenciled on your throw pillows or tattooed on your granddaughter's forearm, but it's dynamite all the same. The same could be said for the loaded comment Paul makes three verses later, "The leaders in Jerusalem added nothing to my message."

Just to review: everywhere the apostle Paul journeyed, preaching the good news of grace alone in Christ alone through faith alone, false teachers followed close behind him, claiming apostolic authority for themselves and teaching a different gospel. Rather than proclamation about what God has done for you free of charge in Jesus Christ, the false teachers issued exhortations about what you must do for God by following the obedient example of Jesus Christ. The false teachers both in Paul's day and in every age have muddled the message of the gospel with the law into a kind of glawspel, a Christ-plus-commandment-keeping antigospel that, as Paul says in chapter 1, is not only no gospel at all, it's anathema, God-damnable. The false teachers compelled non-Jewish believers to undergo circumcision, therefore, because circumcision was the mark of a life lived under the law. Paul responds to the false teachers' aspersions by asserting that his gospel is the only gospel, for his gospel was taught to him by the Risen Christ over a period of three years during a self-imposed exile in Arabia. *My Gospel is authentic because Jesus Christ himself gave the gospel to me*, Paul declares at the end of chapter 1. Here, at the top of chapter 2, Paul insists that the other apostles, James and Peter, affirmed the authenticity of Paul's gospel message when Paul went by revelation to Jerusalem fourteen years into his gospel mission. Affirmed by the apostles in Jerusalem, but also endorsed by the Holy Spirit—that's why Paul takes Barnabas with him to Jerusalem. Barnabas was a Jewish convert to faith in Christ. Barnabas was also an eyewitness to the phenomenon of gentile converts receiving the Holy Spirit when they heard Paul's gospel and placed their faith in Christ and his grace.

So, you see the layers of Paul's rebuttal. My gospel is the only authentic gospel because:

- It was delivered straight from the lips of the Risen Jesus;

- It was affirmed by his other apostles;

- And—just ask Barnabas—it was endorsed by his Holy Spirit.

- And if you don't believe me, if you don't trust my gospel is the gospel, Paul challenges the Galatians. Here's Titus. Titus is a gentile. Go ahead, check under the hood. I took him with me to Jerusalem when I laid my gospel before the other apostles, and they did not compel him to be circumcised, nor did they add anything to my gospel.

The point Paul asserts is that the Judaizers are mistaken in saying not that Jesus Christ is enough without circumcision but that later on down the road we may have to add something else. Say, Jesus plus a contrite, repentant heart, or Jesus plus personal piety, or Jesus plus social justice activism. Paul's point is that Jesus Christ plus nothing else whatsoever, for all time and in every circumstance—Christ plus nothing—is the good news for you. And therefore, to be a Christian requires only that you come to Christ with nothing.

In his preface to his *Commentary on the Epistle to the Romans*, the theologian Karl Barth writes that a true understanding of Paul's apostolic message will always verge on the precipice of heresy.[1] This is because, Barth says, the gospel announces a radical departure from and a seismic rupture with every form of religion. Religion concerns our journey to God and what we do for God. And the gospel is something else entirely. It's the announcement of God's journey to us. It's the promise of what God has done for us. A right understanding of Paul's gospel will always verge on the precipice of heresy. Barth could have had in mind these two verses: "They did not compel Titus to be circumcised" and "They added nothing to my message." If you don't find yourself teetering on the precipice of heresy, with your toes curled over the edge, then you still don't understand Paul's gospel. Because if the message has landed, then your inevitable next questions will verge on the *verboten*. For example, the gospel should provoke you to ask, "Does this mean there's nothing we must do?" Or the even better question, "Does this mean we can do whatever we want?" If the gospel's brought you to the precipice of those two questions, then the true gospel has gotten a hold of you.

Jerry Root is on the faculty at Wheaton College. He's a world-renowned evangelist and widely respected scholar of Christian apologist and Narnia creator C. S. Lewis. In 2017, Jerry Root was invited to deliver a series of lectures at Utah State. During the final lecture, in a crowded auditorium of Mormons and skeptical undergraduates, someone asked

1. Barth, *Commentary*, 25.

Jerry Root how a man as smart as him could be a Christian. Without even pausing to consider the question, as though he knew the truth of it in his bones and carried it with him every day, Jerry Root replied, "I'm a Christian because I know enough of my deficiencies to be devastated. I'm a Christian because I know enough of my goodness to distrust it. I don't think I could live without forgiveness and without the grace of God."[2] In the audience that night was a young mother named Katie Langston who'd grown up in a conservative Mormon family but who was at the breaking point of religious exhaustion. All the *oughts* and *shoulds* of the Mormon religion, all the righteousness-seeking and worthiness-accruing and commandment-keeping, had brought her to spiritual despair. Langston describes hearing Jerry Root's response as a conversion experience. In her memoir *Sealed*, in which she shares her journey out of Mormonism and into the gospel of grace, Langston writes,

> That was it. Dr. Root's reply was a simple one, but I'd never known anyone to admit such a thing out loud. It was the cardinal rule of Mormon spirituality: Be ye therefore perfect, and if you couldn't be perfect, you must do all you can to fix it. Try harder. Get absolution. Pray more. You didn't name your brokenness. You battled it, sought to excise it with every ounce of energy you possessed. To admit powerlessness in the face of your deficiencies was to let your deficiencies win. Yet here was a man, mature and accomplished, who knew the devastation of human brokenness but didn't despair over it. He had a life-line, he said: forgiveness and the grace of God. Could the Christian Gospel possibly be that simple? He admitted his deficiencies in the present tense—he still had them, he hadn't eradicated them—but somehow he was whole anyway. You could see it in the way he spoke of his flaws: he neither relished them nor felt such shame about them that he sought to hide them . . .
>
> *It's not this easy, it can't be this easy*, I thought, but even as I did, I knew it was. The last bulwarks of my resistance [to Christ] crumbled. I could not have anticipated the disruption this would cause to my life and my sense of place in the world, but it didn't matter. All that mattered was that I no longer needed to be other than who I was. My heart sang out, *Yes! I'm deficient. I'm devastated. I'm human at least!*—with each breath, turning myself over to the One who could make of me what I had never been able to make of myself.

2. Langston, *Sealed*, 153.

I say I turned myself over to God. But that's not entirely accurate. It's more correct to say that I was turned; that is, for all those years I'd gotten it precisely backward. I had believed that I must choose God in order to be loved, but the reality what that God's love chose me. In that instant, on the precipice, the world right-sided itself, and I trembled as the foundations of my life fell out from under me, only to discover that I was standing, for the first time, on solid ground.[3]

Nearly three centuries ago, in Middletown, Connecticut, a poor, semiliterate farmer named Nathan Cole experienced a similar gospel epiphany as Katie Langston. In October 1741, Cole heard a sermon by the Methodist preacher George Whitfield, and he later recorded the effect of the gospel on him in his diary. He wrote:

> To me, this is what it means to be a Christian. My hearing Mr. Whitfield preach gave me a heart wound; and by God's blessing, my old foundation was broken and turned upside down. I saw not only that my sins condemned me but that my righteousness could not save me, and I understood finally that if Christ is everything then I have nothing to bring him. Indeed to come to him with this nothing, that is, by faith only, is the essence of what it means to be a Christian.[4]

Notice he didn't say, "I'm going to have to get my turds in a herd now." No, what he said was, "I stopped trusting myself." I ceased trusting in whatever good works of my own I've attempted to add to the gospel. That's what it means to be standing right-side up. It's not just our sins that come between God and us. It's our "goodness." This is what Luther meant in his Romans commentary that the preacher's first task is to eliminate the good for their hearers. Christ has already taken our sins away—they're not the problem. It's holding onto our goodness, thinking it does us any good at all, that keeps us living upside down in the world that Christ has right-sided.

On the precipice between law and grace, the world right-sided itself for Katie Langston. According to the apostle Paul, the problem with those who want to add some obligation other than faith to the gospel, perverting the gospel into a Christ-plus-commandment-keeping gospel, mixing the gospel and muddling it with the Law—the problem with those who want to add to the gospel is that they're insisting on living upside-down in a world that

---

3. Langston, *Sealed*, 154.

4. Stott, *Message of Galatians*, 87.

Jesus Christ has already right-sided. After all, the Bible says the entire purpose of the law is to impress upon you your need for a savior. Think about it. You can't possibly attempt to keep every one of the Old Testament's 613 commandments without being confronted every day by the reality that you cannot do it all, that you are not righteous, that you need a savior. That's why Jesus locks all the exits in his Sermon on the Mount and says that if you've even lusted in your heart, you've committed adultery. He wants to hit you with the truth that you have no hope other than a savior. But that savior has come, taking from you, in his body upon the tree, all your sins, and gifting to you, by the power of his resurrection, all of his righteousness. Therefore, the purpose of the law has been satisfied. The reason for the overwhelming number of commandments has come and gone. It's not that the commandments have been annulled; it's that they've been fulfilled. The world's been right-sided. And so, as the book of Hebrews puts it, the way to honor the law now is to refuse to treat it as religiously valuable. The way to truly keep the commandments now is to abstain from assigning them any saving significance. The way to honor all the *oughts* and *shoulds* of Scripture—including the law Jesus lays down—is to require of believers faith alone apart from any *ought* or *should*. In other words, to require nothing. Christ has come. To believe that your obedience to the law is in any way necessary or even salutary, that it in any way makes you worthy or righteous, to think that your good deeds, even in the slightest, atone for your wicked deeds, is to dishonor the law. It's to refuse to stand upon the solid ground that Christ and him crucified has laid beneath your feet.

You see, it's out of reverence for the commandments that Paul refuses to add them back to the gospel. Christ has already come. The savior has arrived; therefore, the way to honor the law, the way to keep the commandments, the way to be holy, is to do nothing but place your trust in Jesus Christ. Of course, that brings us back to the precipice with our toes curled over the edge of heresy. Do we not have to do anything? There's a difference, Paul wants us to see, between "Must we . . . ?" and "Will we . . . ?" Paul's aside in verse 10 today about remembering the poor is but an indication. As a Christian, you will do many, many things. You will find yourself confessing and repenting. You will forgive the very people you swore you never would forgive. You will give to the poor and befriend companions you'd never choose and engage in issues you once avoided. You'll also sin and self-justify and daily demonstrate your need for a substitute savior. As a

Christian, you will do many things. But to be a Christian, you must do only one thing. Nothing. Just trust in him and his grace for you.

The man with the razor-burned chin and the red parka—he was at an Easter outdoor service during the pandemic. I recognized him in the communion line. When I had placed the elements in his outstretched hands, he'd started to cry and said, "Thank you."

"This is the body of Christ, broken for you," I'd said. "The blood of Christ, poured out for you."

"Thank you," he'd said.

Not "Amen." Not "Thanks be to God." Not even "Happy Easter!" or "Christ is risen indeed!" "Thank you," he cried, like I'd just handed him an ice-cold bottle of pilsner in the desert. Once again, he lingered long after the benediction. His tears glistened in the Sunday morning sun.

"Say," I said, "for someone supposedly teetering on the edge of becoming a Christian, how come I don't see you around much?"

He wiped his eyes on his sleeve. "I've been coming and going from church nearly my whole life. I learned quick that if I come on any ordinary Sunday, then, chances are, I'm going to be given something I gotta do, told who I should be other than the me that's me. But if I only come on Christmas and Easter, I've got a very strong chance of hearing nothing. Nothing but good news."

He shook my hand, still holding the empty plastic pandemic receptacle for the bread and the wine. And as he walked away, I looked down at the ground around me, searching for the keys and coins that surely had spilled from my pockets. Because he had just right-sided my world and set me back again on solid ground.

Cheapened Grace

Galatians 2:15–21

I N CASE YOU WERE wondering, I don't dress in a funny way on Sundays in order to get girls. And I'm not up in a pulpit Sunday after Sunday because I'm an extrovert. Truth be told, I hate public speaking. It's why I never eat before worship. I have felt physically ill every Sunday morning for twenty years this September. I do what I do I because I believe. I really do. Like I recently preached, I don't just believe God raised Jesus from the dead; I know Christ is alive because I've met him. Or rather, he met me. The Risen Christ encountered me and upended my life. I believe. I really do. I believe the Risen Christ is the Crucified Christ who died for me. I believe that he is my full and final forgiveness. I believe his permanent perfect record is mine. I believe he's LORD. I have faith in Christ.

But not always.

The first time I lost my faith I was a second-year student in seminary, and I'd been a solo pastor for three months when a member of my tiny little United Methodist congregation outside of Princeton, New Jersey, went home one Sunday after the ten o'clock worship service, climbed downstairs to his basement, spread out the plastic tarp that was still dirty from a long-ago family camping trip, unlocked the deer rifle with which he'd once taught his son to hunt in the Pine Barrens, sat down in a wrought-iron lawn chair, and with a single flick of the finger he managed to pull down all four corners of the sky onto his family.

His name was Glenn.

Sitting in Glenn's kitchen that Sunday afternoon, I noticed the appointments and to-do's written on a Philadelphia Phillies calendar next to the black rotary phone on the wall.

A shopping list was scotch-taped on his fridge door next to faded 3-by-5 photos and postcards.

He needed eggs and creamer.

I sat there with my hands on the pink formica tabletop acutely aware that I was in no way prepared to do anything for them, not only because I had such little training but also because, suddenly, I had such little faith. In my homily a few days later I said exactly what the family had ordered me to say. You would've thought Glenn had died peacefully in his sleep after a long and happy life. I preached about the importance of faith, about not losing faith in the providential purposes of God, about keeping faith in the love and mercy of God who shares our grief in Jesus Christ. I was about eight minutes into my first-ever funeral sermon when I realized that what I was saying wasn't true. True for me. It felt like my faith had been amputated from me. I could remember what it had felt like to have it as a part of me, and now all I could feel was its not-there-ness. After a while I realized that could be a problem for a preacher. Nothing changed for a couple of months. I didn't know what to do. I thought about dropping out of seminary. I applied to teach school in New York City. I applied to work at a dude ranch in Montana—seriously. I made the mistake of sharing my dilemma with my ordination mentor here in Virginia; he very helpfully suggested that maybe I shouldn't be a pastor after all. I confided to a retired minister who didn't seem to understand and who, without a trace of irony, suggested that if I'd lost my faith I could at least teach at a seminary. What they didn't understand was that I wasn't worried about my career. I just wanted my faith back. That was the first time I lost my faith, but it's hardly been the only time.

It vanished again one afternoon a few years ago. After a year of surgery and seven rounds of "stage-*serious*" chemo,[1] when all was supposed to be on the mend, I was standing in a hotel bathroom that overlooked the Birdland Jazz Club on 44th street in New York City, and I discovered yet another new lump on my body. I turned on the shower and the fan so my kids wouldn't hear me crying, and then I sat down on the cold tile floor and I did what Job's wife dared her husband to do. I cursed God. A few years before I got cancer, I was at opening day for the Washington Nationals with my boys. When we got back home, I got a call that one of my confirmation students, a sixth-grader named Jack, was in the ER at Mt. Vernon Hospital.

"Maybe it's already too late," the neighbor said.

---

1. Micheli, *Cancer Is Funny*. I asked the doctor if my cancer diagnosis had a stage number associated with it, and his response was that I have a unique and fast-progressing form of cancer that isn't diagnosed in traditional stages. He described it as "stage-serious."

When I got there, he was gone. Jack's mom was on the bed with her arms around him, telling him how much she loved him, how much everyone loved him. For I don't know how long, I held Jack's hand and rubbed his hair and tried to get the words out. I tried to tell him how funny and special and alive I thought he was.

"Jason, would you pray?" Jack's mom asked, looking up at me desperately.

And only because I didn't have the heart to refuse her, I prayed. I prayed to the God in whom my faith was suddenly in very short supply.

I share those stories not to be dark or lurid, but because we all have seasons in our lives when, as Bilbo Baggins laments to Gandalf, we "feel thin, sort of stretched, like butter scraped over too much bread"[2] Maybe you're a college student who was recently thrown into the deep end of science and history and philosophy and you can't help but wonder that maybe Christianity is stuck on the shallow side of the pool. Perhaps you just lived through a global pandemic that's killed millions of the world's most vulnerable people and, like Woody Allen, you suspect that God, if he exists, is basically an underachiever. You could be an African American struggling with this faith after seeing so many who share it lured away by the idols of racism and Christian nationalism. You might be a news junkie who has grown disillusioned with the faith after discovering the hypocrisy and greed and abuse and partisanship of so many Christian leaders. Maybe it's as simple as your kids are out of the house, and now you're not so sure if what you thought was faith was actually more of a habit. Unless you are Jesus Christ himself, we all have times in our lives when our faith feels as empty as a dial tone. For many of us, most of the time, our faith feels as fragile as a house of cards. And that might be a very big problem because today the Scripture declares that everything comes down to faith: "Yet we know that a person is not justified by works of the law but through faith in Jesus Christ" (Gal 2:16).

The apostle Paul here is rebutting the false teachers who'd led the churches in Galatia astray from the gospel and convinced them that, having put their faith in Christ's shed blood, their acceptance by God now depended on keeping the commandments. The reason we can never assume the gospel and move on to our preferred topics and personal projects is that even the best of us are attracted to false gospels. As Paul noted earlier in his letter, even Peter—even Peter, the rock on whom Jesus said he would build

2. Tolkien, *Fellowship of the Ring*, 57.

his church—when pressured by the false teachers to add to the gospel, fell away from the true gospel. The apostle Paul's rejection of the false teachers' gospel takes the form of a rebuke of Peter: "We ourselves [as in, you and I, Peter] are Jews by birth and not gentile sinners; yet we know [from our Scriptures and from our personal experience] that a person is justified not by the works of the law but through faith in Jesus Christ."

Justified.

As the Anglican evangelical author John Stott writes, "Nobody has understood Christianity who does not understand this word justification."[3] It's *dikaiosoune* in Greek. It occurs as a verb three times in verse 16 and again as a noun in verse 21. It's a term borrowed from the law court. Justification is the opposite of condemnation. In the Bible, it refers to God's act of unmerited favor by which God puts sinners right with God, not only pardoning them or acquitting them, but treating them as innocent, even as righteous. Justification names God's gracious intervention in Christ to bring us back into alignment with himself. It's about restoration of relationship. Which means, apart from being justified, you and I are not in right relationship with God. No, that puts our circumstances far too benignly. As Paul asks rhetorically in 2 Corinthians 6:14, "What partnership have righteousness and iniquity?" Answer: None. That doesn't square with the watered-down, cotton-candy Christianity of our culture, which basically says God loves and accepts you just the way you are. But the teaching of the Bible, from beginning to end, is that, apart from being justified, we are all under the judgment—the just sentence—of God, alienated from his fellowship and banished from his presence.

Have a nice day.

We all love the verse where Jesus declares that he did not come into the world to condemn the world. We forget the very next verse where Jesus explains that he did not come into the world to condemn the world because the world already stands condemned. That's you and me Jesus is talking about. That this is so means the most urgent question for us is the one Job's so-called friend Bildad asks him, "How then can a mortal be justified before God?" (Job 25:2). The false teachers in Galatia said—and a whole lot of progressive and conservative churches today say—believe in Jesus and do everything God commands and abstain from everything God forbids. In other words, have faith and make yourself righteous by performing the

3. Stott, *Message of Galatians*, 52.

works of the law. This is what Paul refers to in Romans 10 as "seeking to establish a justification of [our] own."

"How then can a mortal be justified before God?"

The false teachers said: Believe in Christ and keep the commandments.

The gospel says: faith.

That's it. Through faith alone you are justified. And only through faith are you justified. Faith is the sole, single, solitary means by which the just sentence of God is lifted from your head. Exclusively by faith does God, who is righteous, accept you, who is unrighteous. Here's my question, and it brings us back to our original dilemma: Is this good news?! Is it a comfort that the gospel takes away all other avenues of being justified and leaves only the narrow door of faith? Does it ease your anxiety at all that Paul takes all the poker chips and pushes them to the center of the table and goes all in on faith alone?

I mean, faith is not a constant for any of us. Faith cannot be forced. We cannot will ourselves to believe something we don't believe. Nor can we prevent doubt and unbelief from overwhelming us like the Nothingness that comes creeping over everything in *The Never-Ending Story*. It raises a long series of questions. If your enoughness hinges on faith only, then is that good news? How do you know if you really have faith? How much faith is saving faith? Is it your faith today that justifies you? Is it faith on your best day that justifies you, or is it your faith on your last day that matters? I get approached by people all the time about redoing their baptism, because they're not certain they really believed when they first believed. But who can ever be certain? The Bible says we see through a glass dimly. We are strangers to ourselves. And what about those people—and there are a lot of them—who want to have faith, who've prayed for faith, but who, for whatever reason, find that faith eludes them? Is it really good news that the gospel takes away the works of the law, good deeds we can do and see done and measure and quantify? Is it really good news that the gospel instead makes our acceptance by God hang on as delicate a thread as our faith in Jesus Christ?

Then again, is that what the apostle Paul is really saying here?

The first time I lost my faith it went missing for months. Eventually, I confessed the dilemma to a theology teacher I trusted, Dr. Darrell Guder. I lingered after class one day.

"You look like a gentleman who has something on his mind," he said, gesturing to me to sit back down.

Dr. Guder had a thick, Magnum, P.I. mustache and the crooked accent of an American who taught in Germany for most of his career. At first I just told him everything I've already said here. I guess what I expected was for him to pull some psychological method from his pastor's toolbox to break my spiritual logjam. I expected an *Ordinary People, Good Will Hunting* sort of breakthrough. Instead he gave me the shortest, most important Bible study of my life.

"I've lost my faith," I told him, wrapping up my story.

And he just smiled and chuckled and patted me on my knee and said, "Don't worry, Jason, it'll come back to you. In the meantime, thank your lucky stars that it's not your faith that justifies you."

It's not your faith that justifies you. He didn't even crack open a New Testament or cite Galatians 2:16, but that ten-second Bible study—for me, it's been like that scene in the movie *Twister*, when Bill Paxton ties himself with his belt to a well as the tornadoes pass all around him. It's been an anchor, and it's held every time. According to most modern translations, it sounds like Paul is saying that it's our faith in Jesus Christ that justifies us. But there's two problems with that understanding. The first problem is that it makes your faith into a work, thereby replicating the Galatian heresy. If it's something we do (faith) that justifies us, then, by definition, we're self-justifying. The second problem with this understanding is that it does not comport with the literal meaning of the text; that is, it's not what Paul says in the original Greek.

Buckle up. You're going to have to do some work now. The relevant words in Greek are *pistis*, *Christou*, and *Iesou*. Now, there is a way in Greek to communicate our faith in Jesus Christ. It's *eis Christon Iesoun*. And Paul knows how to speak of our faith in Jesus Christ because *eis Christon Iesoun* is how Paul puts it in the middle of verse 16: "In Christ Jesus we have believed." But *eis Christon Iesoun* is not the construction Paul uses at the beginning and end of verse 16. In those others instances where Paul speaks of our justification by faith, it's *dia pisteos Christou Iesou* and *ek pisteos Christou Iesou*. Even though many contemporary versions of the Bible get it wrong, any first-semester Greek student can attest to this: in terms of grammar, *pisteos Christou Iesou* is a subjective genitive—meaning, *Christou Iesou* is the subject of the word *pistis*, not the object.

Christ Jesus is the subject of the word "faith." He's not the object. It's a subjective genitive. At the top and bottom of verse 16 today, Paul's referring not to our faith in Jesus Christ but to the faithfulness of Jesus Christ.

Skeptical? Don't believe me? Allow me to phone a friend, a very impressive friend. Listen to the King James Bible: "We who are Jews by nature, and not sinners of the gentiles, knowing that a man is not justified by the works of the law, but by the faith of Jesus Christ, even we have believed in Jesus Christ, that we might be justified by the faith of Christ, and not by the works of the law: for by the works of the law shall no flesh be justified" (Gal 2:15–17). Paul's not saying that it's your faith in Jesus Christ that puts you right with God. Why would Paul say that? That would make you your own savior. Paul is saying that it's the faithfulness of Jesus Christ that justifies you. It's not, "Believe in Jesus Christ and you'll be justified." It's, "In Jesus Christ, you're justified. Believe it!" And of course that's what Paul would say, because his whole gripe with the false teachers over adding works to the gospel is that they've betrayed Christ who alone is the saving work. His work is reckoned to you not as your wage but as a gift. As grace. Paul's entire point is that those whose worry about cheap grace pushes them to add *oughts* and *shoulds* to the gospel actually cheapen grace, because the basis on which God lifts the just sentence against you and accepts you, sinner that you are, is the faithfulness of Jesus Christ. And nothing else. His faithfulness. His faithful life stands in as your own obedience to the Law—as though you yourself had done it. And his faithful death serves as the substitute for your own disobedience—as though he himself had done it. This is why T. S. Eliot called the cross of Christ the still point of the turning world.[4] Because it's the faithfulness of Jesus Christ that puts things right.

Like I said at the top, I've been preaching now for twenty years, long enough to know the question many of you will ask next: If it's the faith of Christ and not my own faith that justifies me, then what good does my faith do? Faith grasps hold of Christ's faithfulness. That's actually the meaning of that middle phrase in verse 16, *eis Christon Iesoun*. Literally, it's "into Christ Jesus we have believed." In other words, faith grabs onto the Faithful One, Jesus Christ. As Martin Luther put it, "faith clings to baptism."[5] What is baptism? Baptism is the faithful work of Jesus Christ applied to you, such that, now, no matter your sin, no matter your doubts and unbelief, no matter your spotty performance as a disciple, no matter if your puny faith makes a mustard seed look like a mountain, by his faithfulness applied to you, through water and the word, you are in Christ now. Believe in that. Put your faith in that. Cling to that. When life sends

4. Eliot, *Four Quartets*, 18.
5. Luther, *Luther's Large Catechism*, 40.

twisters swirling all around you, grab ahold of that. It'll hold. What good is your faith? John Stott answers,

> Faith has absolutely no value in itself; its value lies solely in its object. Faith is the eye that looks to Christ, the hand that lays hold of him, the mouth that drinks the water of life. And the more clearly we see the absolute sufficiency of Jesus Christ's divine-human person and sin-bearing death, the more incongruous does it appear that anybody could suppose that we [with our faith] have anything to offer.[6]

Two years ago, I was about to head home one Sunday after worship when a distraught stranger wandered into the atrium and, in broken English, explained that he was looking for a place to bury his newborn niece. A few days later, outside in the church cemetery, I threw down a fistful of dirt, intoned "earth to earth, ashes to ashes," and made the sign of the cross over her casket. And then I watched and waited and waited and waited as family members pulled her weeping mother away from the short, open grave. If the kingdom had come that afternoon and everything hinged on my faith, the odds were not in my favor. But if everything depends on Christ, on his faithfulness, then I'm pretty confident. Even in my doubt and unbelief, I can be certain.

Hear the good news: If the faithfulness of Jesus Christ is your enoughness before a holy and righteous God—if the faith of Jesus Christ is your enoughness—then you never need to worry about whether or not you have enough faith. Get out of your insides and grab ahold of him.

---

6. Stott, *Cross of Christ*, 138.

Lay Your Deadly Doing Down

Galatians 3:1–9

"OH, YOU IDIOT GALATIANS—WHAT are you doing? How dumb can you be? Why in the world do you think this is the path to a new and improved you?"

William Lyttle was a British civil engineer from Ireland. By the time he died in 2010, Lyttle had become infamous as the "Mole-Man of Hackney." Sometime in the middle of the 1960s, Lyttle inherited a multimillion-dollar estate in the East London borough of Hackney. It was a treasure. And Lyttle didn't work for it or earn it. He didn't buy it with his wages or purchase it on his credit. It didn't cost him a single farthing. He inherited it. By another's death, it was gifted to him.

And what did Lyttle do with his inheritance? How did Lyttle respond to the free gift? Lyttle thought that it was not a proper estate without a wine cellar, so no sooner had he moved into the house than he set upon digging himself a wine cellar. But once Lyttle had begun his work to improve upon his inheritance, he immediately became more interested in his "improvement" project than he was with simply enjoying the gift. He left the gift behind entirely—took it for granted—and became consumed with his work. He didn't stop with a modest wine cellar. A proper estate, he thought, needed connections—to the Tube, to the canal path, and to the local pub. Starting in the mid-60s, with only a hand-shovel and a homemade pulley, Lyttle dug a web of tunnels and caverns and burrows underneath and all around his estate. He dug several levels of tunnels, digging as far down as 100 feet, all the way to the water table. He dug the length of football fields in all directions across the circumference of his house. One of Lyttle's neighbors, Marc Beishon, told *The Guardian* newspaper that they expected him to pop up through their kitchen floor some evening. They could hear him down there, underneath their house, digging and digging and digging. Marc Beishon's wife, Joy, was less amused, telling a reporter that they had moved into their home six years earlier and had been complaining to the town council ever since. The whole neighborhood lost power one day when the Mole-Man dug straight through a 450-volt cable.

Get this: Joy Beishon spoke to a reporter in 2006. Meaning, she moved into her house in the year 2000. Meaning Lyttle, the Mole-Man of Hackney, dug and dug and dug, underneath the mansion that was his inheritance, for over forty years. Forty years! For four decades he worked and worked and worked—foolish, futile work—to improve upon the treasure he was freely given. In 2006, the road that ran in front of William Lyttle's estate cratered and became impassable and the city removed him from the estate and, on the public's dime, they put him up in a hotel apartment. On the top floor. The city eventually removed forty tons of debris from Lyttle's garden. He had dumped still more tunneled earth into the bedrooms of his mansion. It cost the town over 100,000 pounds to fill in the Mole-Man's tunnels with concrete just so the estate wouldn't collapse into the Swiss-cheesed earth below. When a reporter asked the Mole-Man of Hackney if he'd ever kicked back and enjoyed a bottle of wine in the mansion he had inherited, Lyttle rubbed his chin, as if trying to recall.

"He that hath ears to hear, let him hear."

Shooting the breeze one Sunday morning in the narthex—this was shortly after I read about the Mole-Man's death in the newspaper in 2010—I told the story to a parishioner named Lew (bless his heart). Mostly, I figured any time I spent telling Lew a story—any story—would be time Lew was not telling me how I was an incompetent preacher and a terrible pastor and an embarrassment to the United Methodist Church, three of his favorite lines of conversation. Lew had given his heart to Jesus Christ at a Billy Graham crusade decades earlier, he once told me, and ever since he'd poured himself into serving on church committees, signing up for Disciple Bible studies, participating in prayer groups, organizing men's golf trips, serving in soup kitchens, sleeping at hypothermia shelters, going on mission trips, taking spiritual-gift surveys, learning contemplative practices, and all the rest. You name it. He had done it or read it or practiced it. To no discernible effect. Lew was an insufferable cuss about as short on patience and gentleness as he was bereft of self-awareness. And I'm not betraying any confidence because Lew was promiscuous in sharing his low estimation of me. Lew was about the most unsanctified person I've ever met; and, keep in mind, I used to be a chaplain at a maximum security prison filled with murderers and molesters and gang members. To keep his attention off of me, one Sunday after worship in 2010, I told Lew about the Mole-Man of Hackney. When I finished relaying the story, as a sort of coda, I chuckled.

"What are you laughing about?" he asked, glaring at me with his red cheeks and unkempt eyebrows.

"It's just sort of a sad but funny story," I replied.

"I'll tell you what's sad about it," he said in his nasally voice. "What's sad is that I've lived most of my Christian life exactly like that fool."

And I looked at him, surprised by this apparent glimmer of self-understanding.

"I was a fool for thinking that the way I got into the faith was somehow different from the way I was meant to grow in the faith. I left it behind and I exhausted myself, and now I'm not really any different for it."

I was about to minimize what he'd said, "Oh no, you're being too hard on yourself," but he cut me off, jabbing his finger at me.

"I'll tell you what's even sadder," he said, "you've got a whole church full of mole-men. Hell, you've got an entire denomination of mole-men. That's why I keep telling you you're such a terrible preacher. You just tell us to dig more."

And he pointed towards the pulpit. "You just tell us to dig more, when you should stand up there, drag us out of our holes by the feet, and hand over the goods. You should demand we stop digging and take up our inheritance."

Thus far in his epistle to the churches in Galatia, Paul has defended his gospel of grace and his authority to deliver it as the only true gospel. Now, in chapter 3, Paul pivots back to the Galatians whom he has caught red-handed in heresy. "O, you idiot Galatians!" When the gospel of Christ and him crucified was proclaimed to you—and the word Paul uses there in Greek means "graphically displayed"—it became so real to you that it was as if you were there nailing him to his cross. The gospel convicted you, Paul says, and you put your trust not in your moral performance. You put your trust in him, in his faithfulness, and when you did, when you placed your faith in Christ alone, the Holy Spirit came into your life and even began working miracles in your life. But now, having begun with Christ, these false teachers have conned you into going back to Moses. How can you be so stupid?

The gospel, not the law, faith not commandment-keeping, has always been how God has worked righteousness. And Paul, in verse 6, goes all the way back to the beginning, back to Abraham, to prove the pattern. By nothing more than faith, a treasure fell into your lap—a slate forever wiped clean, Christ's own permanent, perfect record, the Holy Spirit of God at work in your life, wealth beyond measure. How could you be so stupid as to leave such a gift behind and go back to digging out a life with the law?

Now, in order to appreciate why the apostle Paul is ripping out his hair and hollering here, you have to understand the false teachers' side of the debate. Their concern was a legitimate one. The false teachers were concerned about the character of Christians. They were concerned about morality, holiness, and improvement. Recently someone approached me after worship and said to me, "Look, I get it. I know I'm accepted and forgiven. I know that Christ is my enough-ness, but how do I get beyond that? How do I actually grow as a Christian?"

Not only is it a good question, it's a question that cuts to the heart of Paul's letter. Because it's one thing that, on Christ's account, God credits your faith as righteousness, but how do you actually grow into living a more righteous life? Or to put it theologically, once you've crossed over the line into faith, how do you progress from being justified (counted as righteous) to being sanctified (holy)?

The false teachers answered that question by saying that you grow in righteousness by doing the law, by keeping the commandments of God in the Old Testament and the law of Christ in the New, by engaging in Jewish rituals like circumcision. The false teachers said that you become a more generous person, for example, by giving to the poor. You become a more forgiving person by working hard to forgive the people in your life. You become a more patient person, say, by sheltering the homeless. Believing the gospel is what makes you a Christian, but doing the law is how you grow as a Christian, the false teachers taught. But Paul responds to the false teacher's answer by saying that they may as well be handing you a shovel and telling you to dig. And dig. And dig. Until it all comes cratering down.

When I worked as a chaplain at the prison in Trenton, New Jersey, I had a colleague named Mohammad who served as the Muslim Imam. Mohammad was from India. Mohammad was stern and humorless. He loved soccer and, inexplicably, the music of George Michael. Inconveniently, Mo-hammad also had a PhD in Christian theology. Know thy enemy.

On day one of my chaplaincy, Mohammad disabused me of my liberal notions that he and I were engaged in essentially the same work. Mohammad made clear that he and I were not pacesetters on paths that led to the same destination.

He shook my hand and said, "As a Muslim, I regard you, a Christian, as a heretic. And as a Christian, if you really are a Christian, you should regard me as such too. I know the prison administration says we are sup-posed to be colleagues, but my goal is to convert as many prisoners as I can, including the Christians."

"Game on," I said, which I should not have said, because it was out of my hands.

Almost all of the Sunday services at the prison were led not by me or one of the other chaplains but by volunteer preachers, pastors, and laity from churches in the area. A couple of months into my chaplaincy, at a staff meeting, I vented my frustration that Mohammad's Islamic prayer services were attracting more and more prisoners—even pulling inmates from our Christian services.

And Mohammad laughed, which he never did.

"You want to know why more men come to the Islamic services?"

"Yeah, I do."

And he leaned across the conference table and said, "All the Chris-tian preachers—they all exhort. They preach about behavior and practice. Obey this, do that, abstain from those things. They preach only the law, but Islam is the religion par excellence of the law. If the choice is between two religions of law, why would they choose the lesser option? Why would they not choose Islam?"

"Huh, you might be on to something," I begrudgingly admitted.

"It's unfortunate for you," Mohammad said, like a pool hustler who suddenly feels sorry for his mark. "These preachers do not understand that focusing on sanctification is not how your New Testament teaches that people actually become sanctified. Muslims believe that we grow and progress by working on our growth and progress, but Christians don't believe that. Christians believe growth comes in an altogether different manner." And then Mohammad flashed a fiendish, schoolyard grin and said, "Of course, I have a PhD in Christian theology, so maybe it's difficult for you to follow me."

"Oh, I understand you just fine," I lied.

I didn't know it at the time, but Mohammad had in mind passages like this chapter in Galatians.

How do you grow as a Christian once you've crossed the line into faith? It's one thing to be counted as righteous. But how do you actually become more righteous? Paul gives us an answer to that question, and it's both radical and radically misunderstood. Notice: in the first four verses, the apostle Paul reminds the converts in Galatia that when Christ and him crucified was proclaimed to them and when they trusted his work for them, the Holy Spirit came into their lives and began to work miracles in their lives. Now notice again: in verse 5, Paul makes the same exact point, but this time he puts it in the present tense: "Does he who supplies the Spirit to you and works miracles among you do so by works of the law or by the word of the cross that elicits faith?"

He puts it in the present tense. In other words, faith in the gospel is how the Holy Spirit continues to work in your life, which incidentally is exactly what Jesus says in the Upper Room in the Gospel of John. The reason Paul calls them idiots is because they've been fooled into thinking that the way they advance in the kingdom is somehow different from the way they entered the kingdom. Paul is beside himself in this letter, not because he's thought-policing their beliefs, but because he's worried they've started down a path of hoped-for self-improvement that will instead prove self-destructive. Paul's point here is that the way you get into the faith is the same exact way you grow a faithful life. There is absolutely no difference between how you become a Christian and how you progress as a Christian. This is a mistake that many, many, many Christians make, including—especially—preachers; that is, we think we're justified by faith in Jesus, but we're sanctified by trying really, really, really hard to live like Jesus. We think we're reckoned righteous by faith, but that we really become righteous by our works—by our doings and disciplines, by our practices and piety.

Paul says, "You idiots! Fools!" The way you enter the faith is the way you advance in the faith. What makes you a Christian is what matures you as a Christian. You become a Christian solely by trusting in Jesus Christ and resting in the sufficiency of his work. You grow as a Christian by receiving the word of faith and resting deeper and deeper in his all-sufficient work for you. How so? Luther's answer lies in his theology of the cross. It happens when the word keeps coming after you in your crosses. In other words, it happens when God sends a preacher to you.

Our sanctification comes by continually revisiting our justification. This is the frame through which Paul would have you understand the fruit of the Spirit in chapter 5 of this letter. If you're struggling with self-control, for example, if you're not a kind person, if you're cynical and joyless, if you're impatient or harsh, if you're not very loving or trustworthy, the way you will overcome those struggles, the way you will heal those deficiencies, the way you will grow is exactly the same way you got into the faith. Once you enter the faith by eschewing all your works and trusting Christ's work alone, you don't then eschew Christ's work and try really, really hard to be a person who is joyful, peaceable, patient, kind, good, faithful, gentle, and self-controlled. No. Put the shovels down. The Holy Spirit works in your life exactly to the degree that you continue to have the crucified Christ graphically displayed to you, Paul says today. The Holy Spirit works in your life by the gospel message being brought to bear on more and more aspects of your life. The path to a newer and newer you, therefore, is not back to the works of the law but to the word of the cross, the word that continually kills in order to make alive.

At the end of 2017, in Charlottesville, at the African American Heritage Center, Ruby Sales, a lesser-known figure of the Civil Rights movement spoke to a capacity crowd. Around the same time the Mole-Man of Hackney began digging his tunnels, Ruby Sales was a black teenage activist in the Deep South. In March 1965, in Lowndes County, Alabama, Sales and some other activists were threatened outside a convenience store by a local shotgun-toting deputy. When the deputy pulled the trigger, Jonathan Daniels, a Virginia Military Institute graduate and Episcopal seminary student, threw himself in front of Ruby Sales. Just a couple of months after the white nationalists' "Unite the Right" march, I heard Ruby tell the crowd in Charlottesville that Jonathan Daniels died in her place: "Jonathan walked away from the king's table. He could've had any position in society he wanted to, but forsaking all of it he came down among us in Selma where we were in bondage and he gave himself for me."[1]

1. As heard at a live event in Charlottesville, Virginia.

Ruby Sales is an Episcopal priest today.

Though many of her comments drew loud applause and approving nods during the event, one of her assertions drew a muted, even hostile, reaction. When asked about the possibility of future white nationalist rallies in Charlottesville, Ruby Sales discouraged confrontation as the means to stop racism.

"Justice," she insisted, "should not be confused with revenge. Any call for justice that does not offer a pathway [to racists] for redemption is revenge, not justice."

When asked how she could have such hope and compassion as to hold out for the possibility of the redemption of white nationalists, how she could even insist upon their redemption, Ruby Sales said this—listen, it's Paul's whole point today about how you grow as a Christian: "Whatever hope and patience I have, whatever compassion I have for ugly white nationalists' redemption, it comes from having heard about my own undeserved redemption Sunday after Sunday."[2]

The way you enter is the way you advance.

The way you get into the faith is the way you grow in the faith.

As much as it pains me to admit, Lew was right all those years ago. Our LORD did not call me, nor did his bride, the church, commission me to tell you to dig. So hear the good news:

You can crawl out from whatever anxious tunnels you are busy burrowing. You can let go of your shovels. You can lay your deadly doings down. And you can simply enjoy your inheritance, for the gospel of Christ Jesus crucified for you is not only a gift; it is God's self-selected means for your growth. God is determined to bring this good news to you, through a preacher, again and again and again, until you believe it. If Almighty God can make the ground around the burning bush holy, God can use the gospel to do likewise to you.

---

2. As heard at a live event in Charlottesville, Virginia.

The Sin-Eater

Galatians 3:10–14

I N HIS DEPICTION OF Christ in the garden of Gethsemane, during the witching hours of Good Friday, the nineteenth-century French painter Eugene Delacroix depicted Jesus not kneeling serenely with folded hands and backlit by soft, celestial light. He instead painted Jesus praying sprawled flat in the dirt, almost writhing, like a terrible ailment had overtaken him, stretching out his arms, anguish in his eyes, his hands open in a desperate gesture of pleading. Delacroix rendered the Father's incarnate Son twisted into a golem of doubt and despair—as though he had been transfigured from God's own righteousness into a totem of God's rejection. Delacroix shows what Paul says. St. Matthew, in his Gospel account of Gethsemane reports that the same Jesus who had boldly predicted his betrayal and crucifixion in the garden confides to his disciples that he is "deeply grieved and agitated." Or, as the original Greek inelegantly lays it out there, Jesus tells them he's "depressed and confused." "Remain here with me and stay awake, for I am so depressed I could die," Jesus says in the literal Greek (Matt 26:36–46).

And then, according to Matthew, Jesus can manage only a few more steps before he throws himself down on the ground, and the word Matthew uses, *ekthembeistai*, means "to shudder in horror, stricken and helpless." In Gethsemane, Jesus is, in every literal sense of the Greek language, scared out of his mind. Or, as the book of Hebrews describes Jesus on the eve of the passion, Jesus is "crying out frantically with great tears" (Heb 5:7). Matthew shows you what Paul says to you today.

Karl Barth says Jesus' prayer in the garden of Gethsemane doesn't even count as prayer because it's not a dialogue between the Son and the Father. It's entirely a one-way conversation, because it's not just that the Father doesn't speak or answer back; it's that the Son only gets an empty dial tone. God's entirely absent from Jesus, as dark and silent to him as the whale's belly was to Jonah. Barth shows what Paul says.

Martin Luther says when Jesus gets up off the ground in Gethsemane there's nothing left of Jesus. There's nothing left of his own humanity. He's an empty vessel—so that, when Jesus drinks the cup the Father will not remove from him, when he drinks the cup of wrath, he is filled completely with us, with our sinfulness. At the well, the woman ran away saying, "Jesus told me everything I'd ever done."[1] In the garden, Jesus walks away, filled and running over with everything we've ever done. Luther shows you what Paul says.

I spent the summer before I started seminary waiting tables in the dining room at this posh, upscale retirement condominium in Charlottesville. Because I was the same waiter for the same folks seven nights a week, week after week, I befriended some of them, especially a couple named Julian and Elinor Hartt. At our wedding, they gave Ali and me a French saucepan in the shape of a heart (which, I later returned for a normal-shaped pot— and still feel guilty about it). Elinor was a famous artist, and Julian was a retired theologian. He'd grown up a preacher's kid in South Dakota, and all through childhood his best friend was a kid who would become Vice President: Hubert Humphrey. Julian had taught philosophy at Yale for a number of years and then, towards the end of his career, he was recruited by the University of Virginia to head their new department of religious studies. When Julian and Elinor found out that their charming, good-looking waiter was not only a graduate of that same religion department but bound for seminary, they were determined to make fast friends with me. On many weekend afternoons or evenings at the end of my shift, he invited me up to their apartment for conversation and sherry, always sherry, which, up to that point in my life, I had only cooked with.

"I would've thought a Methodist of your advanced age would be a tee-totaler," I said, when he offered me a glass for the first time.

"My father was, but I'm free in Christ," he answered in a prairie accent, and then laughed and tapped his cane on the floor.

We talked about UVA and the Methodist Church and William Faulkner. We talked about upbringings and the connections we both had to the Plains States. We talked about the students he had taught who soon would be my teachers. We talked about his wife and the woman I planned

1. Migliore, *Reading the Gospels*, 180.

to make mine. We sat on his patio one afternoon, watching the humming-birds, when I told him how I planned to propose to Ali.

"You sound more troubled by it than enthusiastic," he said, "Usually it takes a few years of marriage before you sound that way about marriage."

And then he laughed, tapped his cane on the cement, and poured himself another draw of sherry.

"No, it's not that I'm not excited," I said. "It's something else I've been struggling with."

"You sound like a man who needs more sherry," he said, pulling out the cork and pouring.

He stared at the hummingbirds, silent in the sun and stubbornly sipping his sherry, waiting for me to unload my burden. So I confessed to him how I had not yet proposed but I had already decided not to invite my father to the wedding. And then I shared with him the why—why I did not want to invite him, the alcoholism and infidelities, the abandonment, and all the broken promises.

"It sounds like you've set your mind on it," Dr. Hartt said when I finished. "So what troubles you?"

"I might have my reasons," I said, "and they might be very good reasons—I think they are—but that doesn't change the fact that I'm supposed to honor my father and mother, aren't I? As much as I think it's a good decision, I can't shake feeling guilty about all the anger and unforgiveness I still carry around with me like sacks of groceries in damp, rain-soaked paper bags."

He took a few sips of his sherry and nodded, and then, without looking at me, he told me a story.

"My father," he said, "as you know, was a prairie pastor. Well, he had a friend, a colleague I suppose you could say, a Norwegian Lutheran pastor named Johan Aasgaard. He eventually went on to become president of Luther Seminary in Minnesota. Anyways, one time, at some conference or another, Dr. Aasgaard told my father about a woman who was in his congregation."

Dr. Hartt looked up at the clouds, thinking, trying to recall.

"You know, I'm not sure now what provoked him to tell my father this story, but I know my father, who was sort of a fundamentalist, loved to argue with nonpietists about the limits of grace."

And Dr. Hartt paused his story to laugh at the memory of his father and take a sip from his short, little glass.

"Dr. Aasgaard had performed this woman's wedding just a few months earlier. She came to see Dr. Aasgaard one afternoon not long after the wedding. 'Dr. Aasgaard, I have to talk with you,' she said, shaking and trembling and crying, 'I must talk to you now.' So he knew she'd come to confess something to him. And he said to her, 'There's a liturgy in the hymnal for someone in your situation.' He opened the book up to Luther's service of confession and absolution from the Small Catechism, and he invited her to kneel there in his office just as he knelt in front of her.

"They began working their way through the ritual, and she confessed to her preacher. She told him that before she had been married or even met her husband, she'd had a relationship with a doctor. She'd become pregnant by the doctor, and the doctor, who wanted nothing to do with a child, pressured her and pressured her and pressured her into having an abortion."

Dr. Hartt stopped and looked at me to make sure I understood.

"Bear in mind, this was in the 1920s. She relented under his pressure and the doctor arranged for a colleague to do it and she had the abortion.

"'That was the end of the relationship with the doctor,' she confessed to Dr. Aasgaard, crying."

And Dr. Hartt continued the story: "When her husband started courting her, she felt like she should tell him what she had done, but she couldn't bring herself to tell him. And when the relationship became serious, she felt like she should tell him what she had done, but she couldn't bring herself to tell him. And when he proposed to her, she felt like she should tell him what she had done, but still she couldn't tell him. And when they got married, every day she felt like she should tell him what she had done, but she could never bear to do it.

"'Now,' she said to her preacher, 'every time he touches me all I can think about is what I've done and how I've betrayed him. And whenever he talks to me, all I can think about is what I'm keeping myself from telling him.'

"When she finished confessing her story," Dr. Hartt told me, "this pastor stood up and placed his hand on her forehead and said to her, 'In the name of Jesus Christ and by his authority alone, I declare unto you the entire forgiveness of all your sins.'

"'She wept for a long while,' he told my father," Dr. Hartt said, "and then she stood up, wiped her eyes dry, and straightened herself up and said, 'Well now, I guess I better go home now and tell my husband this story.'

"And Dr. Aasgaard looked her straight in the eyes and said, 'What story?'"

Dr. Hartt told me that story years before I'd read Paul's announcement that "Christ set us free from the curse of the law by becoming a curse for us."

Martin Luther says that Jesus the Curse is our most tender comfort. In his *Commentary on Galatians,* Luther paints a picture of it. He shows what Paul says:

> Our most merciful Father, seeing that we were oppressed by the curse of the law and held under its power so that we could never have freed ourselves in our own strength, sent his only Son into the world. And the Father said to him, "Become that Peter, the denier. Become that Paul, the persecutor, blasphemer, and cruel executioner. Become that David, adulterer and murderer. Become that sinner, Adam, who ate the fruit in the garden. Become the thieves, who hung from the cross. For a moment, Son, become the person who has committed the sins of every human being. Be sure you pay and satisfy the penalty of them all." Then the law appears and says to Jesus, "I find that you are a guilty sinner and such a great sinner that you have taken on your body the sins of every creature. Thus, I see no sins on anyone but you. Thus, you must die on the tree!" Then the law lunges against Christ and kills him. But in such a way, the entire world is purified and cleansed of all sin. Now, since sin is abolished by this one man, God only sees throughout the whole world, but especially in those who believe, not only cleansing but righteousness. And if there remains some residue of sin, due to Christ's glory that outshines the sun, God is unable to see it.[2]

"I guess I better go home now and tell my husband this story."

"What story?"

"What story?!" Dr. Hartt repeated it, laughing—reveling really—and tapped his cane as applause. I must've looked confused because Dr. Hartt turned to me and suddenly became a teacher again. "Once you've given

---

2. Luther, *Luther's Works,* 143.

the story over to Christ, Jason, there is no story any longer. This is what Christ Jesus does. He takes our narrative up into his narrative. And when we entrust our narrative to him—the abortion, the infidelity, the unbelief, the selfishness and resentment, the prejudice, the words spoken in anger—he absorbs our narrative into his narrative so that he can hand it back to us and say, 'Your sins are forgiven.'

"And pay attention, Jason, in case they don't teach you this in seminary: it's the calling of preachers, lay and ordained alike, to preside at that wonderful exchange.

"What story!?" Dr. Hartt laughed again and raised a glass to a delightful scoundrel in the sky. "That woman went home rejoicing, my father said, and had a long and happy life, because she was no longer carrying her burden around with her—because Christ Jesus was carrying it. If all the sins of the whole world are found in Jesus Christ, Jason, then they are no longer found in the world. If Christ is guilty of all the sins of the world, then we are all totally and entirely free from all our sins."

And then he took a sip of sherry and hummed a few notes of a song that was impossible not to recognize.

It was "Joy to World."

"As far as the curse is found."

I nodded and thought over everything he'd said.

"Did you share that story to tell me I'm forgiven for not honoring my father? Forgiven for my sin?"

"Oh no," Dr. Hartt laughed. "I mean, you are, of course, but my father's friend told that story to him, and my father told that story to me, and now I've told this story to my friend, in order to remind him that his Father has forgiven all of his sins."

I must've blanched.

"You look like a man who needs a drink," Dr. Hartt said, pouring me another sherry.

"Maybe several more," I mumbled.

"That's fine. That's fine," Dr. Hartt chuckled. "God's party doesn't really get going until the sinners show up—isn't that right!?"

Hear the good news.

Whatever your story:

The hurt you can't let go of.

The gossip and backbiting and double-talk.

The forgiveness you withheld until it was too late.

The doubts that linger.

The disappointments you still resent.

The relationship you let fester.

The lies you tell to shroud your addiction.

The truth you're too cowardly to come out with.

The handout you withheld.

The frustration that others aren't as faithful as you.

The gift you gave with strings attached.

The if-bombs you throw down as conditions of your love.

The prodigal you won't welcome home.

The prejudice.

The self-righteousness and sanctimony that feels good for a second—especially when it's about politics—but then it sticks on you like a bad smell on your shoe.

The secret you keep hidden in the dark corner closet of your heart.

Whatever your story—what story?

Christ Jesus has set you free from that story by becoming that story for you.

The Power of Positive Blaming

Galatians 3:15–23

I N 1916, THE SILENT filmmaker D. W. Griffith directed an epic three-
and-a-half-hour movie entitled *Intolerance* that spanned a timeline of
over 2,000 and juxtaposed four parallel storylines, including the passion
of the Christ. An image of God, depicted as a Mother rocking a baby in a
cradle, serves as the segue from one storyline to the next. Upon its release
in 1916, critics noted that one of the unusual characteristics of the film
was the fact that none of the fictional characters had names. Griffith wanted the characters to not be particular people but general types, that is,
they represented all of us. And Griffith wanted the characters to represent
every one of us, because each of the four vignettes in the film portray how,
in the absence of mercy, intolerance and self-righteousness and moralism
beget suffering and violence and sin.

In the second storyline of the film, the passion of Christ, Griffith
focuses on how those who are obedient to the law react when Jesus of
Nazareth pardons a woman caught in adultery. After the Pharisees have all
dropped their rocks, Jesus recklessly refuses to condemn her. In the film, it's
that moment of uncondemnation that provokes Christ's passion. In their
zeal for God's law, God's people cannot tolerate God-in-the-flesh, so they
push him out of the world on a cross.

At the end of *Intolerance*, Griffith shows this same crucified Christ
returning in glory, and Jesus comes not to the good or the righteous but
rather to those the good and the righteous can least tolerate. Christ comes
to the Big House, full of hardened, guilty-as-hell convicts dressed in black-
and-white prison stripes. As the prisoners look up at the crucified Christ
descending to them—for them—the prison walls begin to fall, their chains
come unbound, their stripes fade away, and they emerge, every last single
prisoner, into the absolving light of a graceful God.

In one of his sermons to the inmates at the Basel prison in Switzerland, Karl Barth preached[1] that the Christian who knows the gospel of grace is like a freed man running up and down the jailhouse halls, hollering to his fellow prisoners that the cell doors have been thrown open, the guards have all gone home, and the warden has been put into permanent retirement and is now fishing in Florida.

"The law imprisoned all things under the power of sin . . . Now before Christ came, we were imprisoned and guarded under the law" (Gal 3:23).

Here's the question: If Jesus is the getaway driver God sends to tunnel under the fence, dynamite the doors, and bust us all out of the prison, then why does God give the law in the first place? Why does God bother giving all those commands if Christ comes to set us free from them? If Law-keeping is not at all what it means to be a Christian, then why do the Father and the Son engage in so much legislative folderol?

"Why then the law?"

To those who insist that believers must add the law onto the gospel, Paul argues that rather than go back to Moses, you should go back to the very beginning of covenant history.

It starts with Abraham, not with Moses. And the covenant with Abraham, Paul notes, is not an if/then conditional contract like the covenant with Moses on Mount Sinai. The covenant with Abraham is more like an irrevocable last will and testament. There are no *thou shalts* or *thou shalt nots* in the covenant with Abraham. There's only God's *I will, I will, I will*. It's an unconditional promise to which the only response is trust—faith. Faith in the promise of Abraham's seed, and Paul claims here that seed refers not to all of Abraham's innumerable descendants but to the incarnate deity. Jesus Christ is the singular seed through whom God will bless the whole world. That's the promise to Abraham, Paul says today. And Abraham believed God's promise, the book of Genesis reports, and God reckoned Abraham's faith as righteousness. You see, Paul's arguing, you don't need to go back to Moses, you don't need to mix the gospel with the law, muddling it into glawspel, you don't need to accrue righteousness by keeping the commandments. Go back to the beginning. Faith alone in the promise of Christ has always been how God has worked righteousness.

And this is the point at which Paul anticipates the false teachers' rebuttal. Why then the law, Paul? You've so fused Christ with Abraham that you've squeezed out Moses. There's no room for the law in your gospel. Paul

---

1. Barth, *Deliverance to the Captives*, 37.

responds to their anticipated question with a surprising answer. The purpose of the law is not to make righteous; the purpose of the law is to reveal.

For a number of years, I was involved heavily in the United Methodist mission in Cambodia, helping to plant churches across a country relatively untouched by the gospel. Because of the genocide perpetrated by the Khmer Rouge regime, Cambodia has one of the world's youngest populations, many of whom first come to Christ through the English classes offered by churches. About ten years ago, I was sitting in my supposedly moisture-wicking REI wardrobe on the floor of an open-air sanctuary hours into rural Cambodia. Rice paddies and water buffalo surrounded the church. Sweating in the cold shower earlier that morning, I had cursed my decision to come to Cambodia, and now I was so hot I could feel my heartbeat in my teeth. But I was supposed to be teaching a Bible class to a horde of twenty-something new Christians.

"My name is Jason," I'd said as simply as I could for these fledgling English speakers. "I'm a pastor in America, and I've come all this way to Cambodia, and further still to your village, well, because Jesus commands me to go and make disciples and commands me, even, to serve the poor."

Next, they went around and each gave their names and shared how long they'd been a Christian. And then, I started teaching them as best I knew about the Sermon on the Mount—my assignment. I unpacked the context for them and pointed out the parallels Matthew draws between the Sermon on the Mount and Mount Sinai, and finally I started working my way with them through Jesus' sermon. I'd read a verse, rephrase it for them, and ask what they thought it meant. So I read Matthew 5:16, "Let your light shine before others," rephrased it, asked what they thought it meant for them, and someone raised their hand and took a stab at understanding it. I read Matthew 5:23, "If you're about to make an offering at the altar and you remember that you've sinned against a brother or sister, lay the offering down, go reconcile with them, and only then come back to offer your gift." I rephrased it, asked what they thought it meant, and waited for a hand to go up. I did that verse by verse by verse without a hitch. Until we got to what Jesus says about adultery, "You have heard it said, 'You shall not commit adultery.' But I say to you that everyone who looks at a woman with lust has already committed adultery in his heart."

Evidently, they'd not yet learned the word adultery in their church-sponsored English classes, so I awkwardly defined it for them using animal husbandry as a safe illustration. Then I rephrased the command for them and, before I asked them what they thought it meant, I told them to look at it again. "Notice," I said, "how Jesus expands the command from action to intention. Jesus says you'll be judged by God not simply on the basis of what you do or fail to do. Jesus says you'll be judged for what's in your heart when you do it. It's not just your outward obedience that matters; it's your inward motivation too. What do you think that means?"

A young man with parted black hair and a Justin Timberlake T-shirt raised his hand and answered, tentatively, "It mean . . . if you [and he pointed at me] only come to Cambodia because Jesus tell you to and not because you really want to, then Jesus say it like you not come here at all. Jesus say you will be judged. Do you think that's right? What do you think?" he asked me.

"I think you speak very good English," I said.

Just then, another student raised her hand. I nodded in her direction and she asked, "Have you ever . . ." And I could see her turn the strange word over in her mouth like a brand new Rubik's Cube. "Have you ever lusted in your heart?"

"Have you seen my wife?! Of course not." I lied.

Class time ran out before we got to the very worst law in Jesus' Sermon on the Mount, the most terrifying command in all of the Bible: "Be perfect, as your Father in heaven is perfect."

The purpose of the law is not to improve you.

The purpose of the law is to accuse you. To indict you and convict you.

As John Stott writes, "Satan would have us to prove ourselves holy by the law which the LORD gave to prove us sinners."[2] Why then the law? The apostle Paul gives two answers. Firstly, the law was "added because of transgressions" (Gal 3:16). Or, as Paul puts it in his Epistle to the Romans, "through the law comes the knowledge of sin" (Rom 7:7–9). In other words, the law functions like the CT scans I undergo every quarter that reveal the current status of my lymphoma. The law makes a visible transgression out of our invisible rebellion. The law is like a plumb line from heaven. It cannot make straight the walls; it can only reveal the crookedness of them.

Will Willimon recently told me that when he's teaching his students at Duke about grace he likes to challenge them to commit that during the

2. Stott, *Message of Galatians*, 79.

course of the semester they will not have sex with anyone to whom they're not married.

I laughed and he explained, "When it comes to woke, well-behaved, inclusive, self-actualized, social-justice-minded Bernie Bros and Gals, I just don't know any better way to acquaint them to the reality that they're sinners other than by telling them it's unlawful for them to have sex outside of marriage."

The law is like a plumb line from heaven.

Secondly, the law is like a holy hand grenade, an almighty molotov cocktail, an accelerant. The law doesn't just illuminate your sin. The law intensifies your sin. As Paul puts it in Romans 5:20, "When the law came in, the trespass multiplied." "The law aroused sin in us," Paul writes in Romans 7, "in order that sin might be shown to be sin, and through the law might become sinful beyond measure." This is what Paul means in verse 23 that "before Christ came, the law imprisoned everything under sin." Martin Luther summarized this verse by saying that "the purpose of the law is to make us not better but worse."[3]

Before his 1916 silent film, *Intolerance*, D. W. Griffith directed the 1915 box office hit, *The Birth of a Nation*. *The Birth of a Nation* was condemned by many critics, protested by the NAACP, and boycotted by some theaters for the racist tropes Griffith used in depicting African Americans and for the heroic light he seemed to cast upon the Ku Klux Klan.

Griffith made no bones about telling people that he intended *Intolerance* to be essentially a celluloid middle finger to all those who had protested and condemned *The Birth of a Nation*. Griffith not only denied the criticisms, he used *Intolerance* to argue that those who protested *The Birth of a Nation* were the real bigots. In fact, he financed the record-setting budget of *Intolerance* himself, which broke him financially for the rest of his life. And long after everyone had stopped caring about his 1915 film, Griffith kept on justifying himself and his problematic production—so much so, he eventually lost his marriage. And then he lost his family. He died alone. And no one—no family or friends, no cast-members or business partners—attended his funeral. The law, like a plumb line, revealed the crookedness in him. But then the law, like an arsonist's gasoline, accelerated it.

The trespass multiplied.

"Why then the law?"

3. Luther, *Luther's Works*, 24:122.

Paul answers that the law is a plumb line from heaven, and the law is a holy hand grenade. But, but, but—why? Those answers just elicit a bigger question.

Why would God give commands for righteousness if those commands only reveal and replicate our unrighteousness?

Prior to the pandemic, I liked to do much of my work at coffee shops. Exactly eight years ago, I sat down at a little round table at Starbucks and I started to sketch out a funeral sermon. At the table to my right were two middle-aged women. They had Bibles in zippered carrying cases on the table along with a copy of the local paper. I don't think I could properly be accused of eavesdropping considering just how loud the two women's conversation was. Like they wanted to be heard. Their "Bible study," or whatever it had been, was apparently over, because the woman by the window closed the Bible and then commented out loud: "I really do need to get a new Bible. This one's worn out completely. I've just read it so much."

Not to be outdone, the woman across from her parried, saying just as loudly: "I don't know what I'd do if I didn't spend time in the word every day. I don't know what people do without the LORD."

"They do whatever they want," her friend by the window said.

They continued chatting over their lattes as the woman by the window flipped through the paper. She stopped at a page and shook her head in disapproval. I can't be sure whether she actually said "Tsk, tsk, tsk," or if I imagined it. The other woman looked down at the paper and said, "Oh, I heard about that. He was only thirty-one."

"Did you hear it was an overdose?" the woman by the window said like a kid on Christmas morning.

And that's when I knew who they were gossiping about. I knew because I was sitting next to them writing that young man's funeral sermon.

"Did he know the LORD?" the woman asked.

"Probably not, considering the lifestyle," the woman by the window said without pause.

They went on gossiping from there. They used words like "shameful." They did not, I noticed, use words like "sad" or "tragic" or "unfortunate." It wasn't long before the circumference of their conversation spun its way to encompass things like "society and what's wrong with it," how parents need to pray their kids into the straight and narrow, and how "this is what happens when our culture turns its back on God." After a while they came to a lull in their conversation and the woman opposite the window, the one with the gaudy bedazzled cross on her neck, gazed down at the paper and wondered out loud, "What do you say at a funeral like that?"

And without even looking at them, and with a volume that surprised me, I said: "The same damn thing that'll be said at your funeral."

They didn't even blush. But they did look at me awkwardly.

"I hardly think so," the woman by the window said, sizing me up and not looking very impressed with the sum of what she saw.

And so I laid my cards down, "Well, I probably won't be preaching your funeral, but I will be preaching his." And then I pointed at her worn Bible, and I said, "I don't know that as well as I'd like, but I do know it says, 'Judge not lest ye be judged,' just as I know it says, 'There is no distinction between any of us, for all fall short . . .' In fact, that book says that apart from Christ's work for you, you're no better than that guy over there." and I pointed to a homeless guy who reeked of dope and booze and was nursing his coffee and muttering to himself. They both stared at me indignantly and then rose, shoving their chairs out from the table, turned up their noses at me, zipped up their Bibles, and stormed out, muttering something about how preachers are supposed to be nice.

About a week later, though, I got a card in the mail—I still use it as a bookmark.

"Pastor Micheli," the letter began, "I'm the woman you spoke to at Starbucks last week. I hope that rings a bell. I hope you don't spend every day eavesdropping on people and then laying the law on them like you did me, but, in my case, I'm so grateful you did. I want to thank you for blaming me, for showing me my sin. When you've gone to church your whole life and when you never stray very far from the flock, it can be easy to miss just how horribly you still fall from the glory of God. I think I've always subconsciously justified myself, telling myself, 'Well, at least I'm better than that person.' Or, I've told myself, 'I'm basically a good person.' But better is not perfect. And basically good is still not good enough to go before a holy God. What I mean to say is this: I've been a Christian my whole life, but I never knew what it meant to throw myself on his mercy—I believed in him, sure, but I never clung to him as my only righteousness—until you held the mirror up to me. Now I feel free, and I realize that, before, I felt anything but. Thank you for not being nice."

God's grace begins where you end.

But God's grace does not begin until you end.

It's not that we can't improve. It's that better is not perfect. For the living water of Jesus Christ to do its work, it needs a vessel that knows it's empty. Jesus is your gracious getaway driver, but you're hardly riding shotgun even. You're rolled up in a carpet in the trunk of the car, dead in your trespasses. As Luther puts it in Thesis 18 of the Heidelberg Confession: "Unless we completely despair of ourselves, we cannot merit the mercy of Christ."[4] The purpose of the law is to drive you to total despair so that you will yield once and for all to total dependence, because what God has wanted from the very beginning of it all is relationship. The Protestant Reformers called law and gospel "God's two words." The first word, law, kills so that the second word, gospel, can make alive. God's word is like a hitman and a midwife. The law of God says do not misuse the name of the LORD. The law also says we misuse his name every time we praise him in here when there's poverty or injustice out there. Remember the sabbath and keep it holy—were you in worship last Sunday? Honor your father and your mother. Do not kill. Do not steal or lie or covet. Do not gossip or talk about another behind their back (how do you score on that one)? Welcome the illegal immigrant in your land and love them as you love yourself. Love your enemies. Turn the other cheek. Forgive upwards of seventy times seven. Sell everything you own and give it to the poor. Do it all with nothing but pure motives. Be perfect, as perfect as your Father in heaven.

Do you hear that as a doable Honey-Do List?

Or do you hear it as exposing how you fall short?

If it's the former instead of the latter, I'll pray for you. And I'll get back in the pulpit and go at it again for you. But if it's the latter, hear God's other word. Hear the good news: the law can only condemn those who rely on their performance of it. If you know you're a sinner and have no hope but the blood of Christ, then you are righteous. If you put your trust in him, if you dare to step out into the absolving light of this gracious God, then you will be holy even in your sin.

---

4. Forde, *On Being a Theologian of the Cross*, 68.

Critical Grace Theory

Galatians 3:23–29

DURING THE FIRST WEEK of Advent in 1977, two weeks after the theatrical release of *Close Encounters of the Third Kind,* a pastor from Immanuel Lutheran Church, Missouri Synod drove his way cautiously through an early winter blizzard to Lima Memorial Hospital in northwest Ohio. Like Nicodemus, the pastor came in the dead of night. In secret. A small, determined grandmother met the pastor at the elevator outside the maternity ward. Spying the clerical collar beneath his winter coat, she introduced herself and then led him back to the new mother's room. With a small, silver pitcher and a pink, plastic bedpan—he'd brought the one, a harried nurse had provided the other—he prayed over the water, "Pour out your Holy Spirit to bless this gift of water and him who receives it, to wash away his sin and clothe him in Christ's righteousness."

And then he asked the two of them, mother and grandmother, the confession of faith, culminating in the final question: "In accepting the responsibility for this child, you are bearing witness publicly that this child has been baptized and that God is creating in him saving faith. It is your responsibility then, henceforth, to remind him of his baptism. Do you intend gladly and willingly to assume this responsibility?"

As prompted, they answered him, "Yes, with the help of God."

And then he baptized me.

I didn't grow up in a religious home. Save for a single, shotgun wedding, I had never before been inside a church. When I was seventeen I was encountered by the Risen Christ—as real and alive as you are to me right now—and I put my faith in him, and I became a Christian. But I was baptized as a baby, because it was important to my mother and to her mother, and they both feared that my father, who is not a believer, would stand in the way. So that pastor came in the middle of the night and secretly baptized me into Christ.

Or, as the apostle Paul puts it today, the pastor put Christ on me.

I only learned that story in the last year. I never thought to ask my mother about my baptism, but when I finally did ask she told me that story. As soon as she did, a memory I vividly recalled but never quite understood clicked into place for me. I remember I was sitting on my driveway playing with my G. I. Joe action figures. My grandma was pulling weeds in our flowerbed. I know I was in kindergarten because we only lived in that house for a year. So I was five years old. It was trash day. Our gray garbage cans were curbed. I was staging a surprise attack of the Joes against Cobra Commander's secret base when the garbage truck pulled up in front of our house. The guy hopped off the back and started rolling the cans to the truck and, for whatever reason, I pointed at the garbage man and I said, "He's a —"

And I used the N-word.

I don't know if he heard me over the truck's diesel rumblings, but my grandmother heard. I didn't even see her get up. Before I noticed her standing over me, she smacked me—hard—across my face and then, in that whisper-yell that only grandmas can really do, she said, "You've put on Christ. Don't you ever talk like the devil with Christ on you."

I never forgot that moment, but I never understood it, not until my mother told me about my baptism last year.

But why had I done it? How do you explain racism on the lips of a kindergartner? I grew up in a family where that word was never thought so much as spoken. Nevertheless, that foul word ended up on my five-year-old lips. I had a toy in one hand and, with the other hand, I had pointed my finger at a black man and I had drawn a distinction between him and me. And distinctions are always appraisals of worth. How do you account for prejudice present in such a tiny person? My peers? Maybe. Their parents? Possibly. The media? Perhaps. But, according to the apostle Paul none of those potential explanations are big enough. They're insufficiently supernatural. According to Paul, none of the -isms that divide and oppress—racism, classism, sexism—can be understood properly apart from the gospel of grace, because they're not simply character flaws or impoverishments of education.

They're powers.

"The law was our disciplinarian," Paul writes, "until Christ came, so that we might be justified by faith." This gets at one of Paul's chief arguments with the false teachers in Galatia. By muddling the gospel with the law, the false teachers have misconstrued the transitory nature of the law. Their glawspel message obscures the fact that the purpose of the law was temporary. The gospel is not simply the arrival of another word; the gospel is the arrival of a new age. "But now . . . ," Paul writes in verse 25.

Paul loves big buts.

In all of his letters, this adversative phrase ("but now . . ") signals the change in situation that occurs on account of the apocalypse of Christ. "But now . . ." signals the turning of the ages that arrives with the advent of the messiah, from the old aeon to the new. "But now . . ." signals the transformation of identity and belonging that comes through faith in the gospel, from the Old Adam to the New Adam.

Paul loves big buts.

Here the apostle uses "But now . . ." to insist that, on account of Christ and by faith alone, what we are is altogether different from what we were. We were under the power of sin. But now we are in Christ. "But now," Paul declares, "as many of you as were baptized into Christ have clothed yourselves with Christ. Therefore, there is no longer Jew or Greek, there is no longer slave or free, there is no longer male and female; for all of you are one in Christ Jesus." Now notice: there are only two sides to Paul's big but. That is, according to the apostolic gospel, there are only two options for describing the reality of everyday life for every single soul under the sun. Either you are under the power of sin or you are in Christ. You're either under the power of sin, or you're in Christ. That's it. There's no room for a third agnostic option: "Well, I'm not a believer, but I'm basically a free and good person." No, and this is because the power of sin is a power. Either you have been delivered by Jesus Christ, clothed with his righteousness and incorporated into him, or you are a subject under the dominion of a power determined to separate you from the love of God in Christ Jesus our LORD.

There's no third possibility, because the power of sin is a power. An agency at odds with God. Just after this section of his letter, Paul calls these powers "the elemental spirits of the world" (Col 2:20). To the church at Corinth, Paul calls such power, simply, the enemy. Writing at the end of his Epistle to the Ephesians, Paul warns, "our struggle is not against enemies of flesh and blood, but against the cosmic powers of this present darkness" (Eph 6:12). In the four Gospels, Jesus refers to this power, alternately, as Satan, Lucifer, the Prince of Darkness, and the Father of Lies. Now, as a good liberal American, I've been reliably informed that Jesus supposedly came to be a good example, teach us helpful life lessons, and to encourage us to work for social justice. However, the apostle John says, as clear as it is inconvenient, "The reason the Son of God appeared was to destroy the works of the devil" (1 John 3:8). As we acknowledge at baptism, all of Christ's activity is a conflict with the devil, and all those who are in Christ are conscripted into this conflict even as they are being contested over. "Do you renounce the spiritual forces of wickedness?," we ask at the font. Yet, even as I use this language, I can see some of your sphincters tighten in embarrassed discomfort. After all, we're sophisticated, modern people. We go to doctors for our healing. We go to Facebook for our news. At least half of us trust scientists. We have experienced what the sociologist Max Weber called de-magnification.[1] Our world has been disenchanted. Our Scripture has been demythologized. And many of us are busy deconstructing our faith. The devil? Please! We're well-educated, modern people.

Despite the fact we can no longer even agree on the truth of an event we've all seen with our own eyes, like the insurrection at the Capitol, we're much too enlightened, we tell ourselves, to believe in an outdated, premodern myth like the Father of Lies. You may not believe in the principalities and powers, but Jesus did. And there's the rub for all of us functional atheists. You can't really call Jesus your LORD while also calling him a liar. So we're stuck with the Bible, and, according to the Bible, there is another unseen agency at work in the world.

But now! Faith has rescued us out from under the power of sin and into Christ Jesus where "there is no longer Jew or Greek, there is no longer slave or free, there is no longer male and female . . ." Karl Barth says that just as we know Christ by his benefits, we know Satan by his detriments.[2] Meaning, under the power of sin, there is Jew or Greek, slave or free, male and female. It's under the dominion of sin that we make distinctions.

In twenty years of ministry, I've only withheld the sacrament of holy communion a few times from a couple of people. One of the lay leaders in my first congregation in New Jersey was a retired teacher and principal named Sheldon. Every Sunday, Sheldon dressed in a three-button suit, bright bow tie, and tortoise shell glasses. Sheldon never missed a Sunday and always brought with him the man with whom he'd lived unmarried for decades. Sheldon frequently volunteered to help serve communion. Not long after the bishop appointed me there, I noticed that Kim, a middle-aged woman with a long brown ponytail, two kids, and, seemingly, an axe to

1. Stott, *Message of Galatians*, 103.
2. Barth, *Deliverance to the Captives*, 144.

grind on any number of issues, would hop out of the communion line and duck into a different communion line, pulling her kids along behind her, every time she was in line to receive the body or the blood from Sheldon. By no means was this church large enough for her demonstration to go unnoticed, and certainly not by Sheldon.

I spoke to Kim about it one Sunday after church. She listened and nodded, and I thought, "Wow, I'm pretty good at this pastor gig." And then the next Sunday it was like her feet were asleep—pins and needles—she exited Sheldon's communion line and entered mine like she was walking through wet cement, aware every eye in the congregation was trained on her. After church, I sent another lay leader, Bob, to talk to Kim. Reporting back to me, Bob seemed as impressed with himself as I had been, so I wasn't all that surprised when, the following Sunday, Kim waited until she was only two people from the front of Sheldon's communion line and then, so everyone behind her could see, darted into my serving line with her two kids in tow. I confronted her in the narthex after everyone had spilled out onto the church lawn. Kim bit her lip and, with her cheeks blushing red, said, "I refuse to receive communion from someone like him." And she pointed through the church doors down at Sheldon who was holding Dan's hand.

"What do you mean 'someone like him?'" I asked.

"Just look at him!" she said, exasperated, "He's . . ." And she was about to say something worse. "He's a sinner."

"I hate to break it to you, Kim, but so are you." Her eyes lit up like she was possessed. "There's no difference between him and you or me. This table is for sinners only. What makes the body and the blood grace is not the sinner who serves it but the word of God attached to it."

She was shaking her head, refusing to concede my point. So I laid down the law.

"If you're going to make a mockery of the meal by refusing to receive from certain types of people, then, until you repent, I'm going to withhold the sacrament from you."

"What?! You can't do that!"

"Yes, I can. And I will. Exactly what do you think my job is here? I'm not a maitre d' or a cruise ship director. I'm a pastor. I'm responsible for your salvation."

She was fuming and actually stomping her feet.

"Look at the bright side," I said, "I could be doing you a favor. St. Paul says that if you receive the bread and the wine unfaithfully, it could kill you."

And, okay, maybe that last line was a bit too heavy-handed, but I think I only made one mistake in dealing with Kim. I treated her like a problem person. I did not treat her like a person under the power of a power.

You're either under the power of sin or you are in Christ. There's no third option because the powers and the LORD Jesus Christ are in conflict—what Paul calls spiritual warfare—and there's no neutral territory. Like the Israelites in the desert drawn back to slavery under Pharaoh, even those of us who are in Christ are not immune from the pull of the powers. Martin Luther says we are all, at once, simultaneously in Christ and under the power of sin.[3] And, like Tolkien's ring, that power has a desire, an aim. And we can identify the intent of the powers because we know the effect of being rescued from them. The effect of God's grace in Jesus Christ, Paul says today, is the destruction of all the world's antinomies—race, class, and gender.

Jew and Greek.

Paul's already told you at the beginning of his letter that "Jew" and "Greek" are racial distinctions every bit as fraught then as "black" and "white" are now.

Slave and Free.

In Paul's day, over half of the world's population were on some spectrum of slavery. "Slave" and "free" are class distinctions. "Male" and "female," those are gender distinctions, and gender distinctions have always been about power.

Grace is the destruction of the world's antimonies.

Why? Because they're hierarchies. They're human systems of merit. Which is to say, they are our attempts to be our own saviors. Now, if the Bible testifies that all of Christ's work is a conflict with the power of sin, and if the word of God says that the effect of Christ's work of grace is the demolition of the world's antinomies, then that means it is the devil's desire to take the distinctions in creation (black and white, male and female, rich and poor, gay and straight) and turn them into divisions so that those divisions turn into oppression.

The spiritual forces of wickedness.

That's how racism ends up in a five-year-old's mouth.

3. Luther, *Luther's Works*, 24:170.

Kim disappeared for a few months, every so often lighting up the grapevine with tales of my coarse insensitivity. But then one Sunday after Easter she came to worship by herself, sat in the back, and finally made her way down the maroon carpet holding her hands out like a beggar.

She looked emptied of some power.

"The body of Christ, broken for you," I said.

Then she dipped it into the cup Sheldon was holding at my side.

"The blood of Christ poured out for us," I heard Sheldon say.

And she didn't respond, "Amen." She coughed out an apology, "I'm sorry."

After worship, on the front steps of the church, I asked Kim if she'd repented. She shook her head.

"No, I didn't repent, I was . . ." And she grasped for how to put it. "I was repented."

And she looked almost afraid, chastened with a holy fear.

"What do you mean, you were repented?"

And she explained: "I prayed and I prayed and I prayed about it. Honestly, I prayed for Jesus to change your mind. But then God answered me. I'd never heard God say anything to me before." And she paused, "I'm not sure I ever want to hear him say anything again."

"What did God say to you?"

"It's like God said to me, 'Sheldon's put on Christ. He's wearing the same thing as you. How dare you see him as any different from you. Stop making distinctions I died to defeat. You're only aiding the enemy,'" Kim said, looking almost traumatized by the reality of the Living and Loquacious God breaking into her life.

There is a will that wills in our world that is not the will of God.

If that's true, if what the word of God says about the spiritual forces of wickedness is true, then not only is it unbiblical to insist that something like racism is a power in which you do not participate, and it is a lie to suppose that some other ism is a problem that can be solved by reading the right book or supporting a certain policy or voting a different way. If it's true that there is a will that wills in our world that is not the will of God and its desire is to divide us, then racial bigotries and class resentments and cultural antagonisms and partisan hatreds and all the rest, they are powers that cannot be overcome.

There is no hope.

Unless God has raised Jesus Christ from the dead.

My youngest son, Gabriel, recently attended a two-week theology program for youth at Shenandoah University. It's one of the perils of being theological offspring. We joined Gabriel for the program's closing worship service in the chapel. The service was a good example of why I make it a point to avoid clergy meetings and denominational gatherings. Nevertheless, I'm happy to report that I behaved. I did not mutter under my breath. I sighed audibly only three times. My wife, though, once the Great Thanksgiving finished with seemingly no awareness that Jesus' meal with his friends ended badly for all of them, leaned over to me and whispered in my ear, "This is so progressive I think maybe they've progressed clear past Christianity." For example, during the service the word Father was conscientiously omitted from the LORD's Prayer, as was the word "kingdom." It was changed to kin-dom—because we all know families are less problematic than monarchies. The preacher made no mention of Jesus in the sermon, while the communion prayer dwelt more on God's dream (whatever that means) than on Christ's cross and resurrection. Meanwhile, the prayers all stressed the imperative of being open and welcoming to difference, so long as the people we are welcoming also listen to NPR, watch Rachel Maddow, and think and vote the same way we do. The liturgy was like progressive Christianity on steroids, which is to say it earnestly gestured towards inclusivity while also being as exclusive and homogenous as the aisles of Whole Foods or the fitness equipment at Orange Theory.

But then, we came to the table. And I ate and I drank—corn arepas and yellow passion fruit juice, but never mind that. As I turned around from the altar to return to my appropriately and hygienically socially distanced seat, I saw that behind me in the communion line was a teenager, a sibling of one of the participants. He was wearing a red Make America Great Again cap and a black T-shirt that said in a big, gaudy, in-your-face-font, "Preserve the Second Amendment." I looked at him and I thought to myself, "Isn't that just like the Living God? Isn't that just like Jesus to look—with grace—upon the sinful way we draw lines and make distinctions and attempt to facelift his body so it looks and thinks just like us? Isn't it just like Jesus to send someone like that MAGA-wearing kid to receive the body and the blood from a woke pastor wearing a 'Love is love is love . . .' T-shirt?" Not only is it just like Jesus. In a world where there is a will that wills that is not the will of God, it's our only hope.

With the Grain of the Universe

Galatians 4:21–31

C LARENCE JORDAN WAS A farmer, Southern Baptist minister, and Greek New Testament scholar whose colloquial paraphrases of Scripture inspired the production of the musical *The Cotton Patch Gospel*. Two decades before the climax of the Civil Rights Movement, in southwest Georgia, Clarence Jordan founded the Koinonia Farm, an interracial Christian farming community. Koinonia is the word the apostle Paul chooses to describe both the mystery of the sacrament and the mystical body of believers who live according to the new age wrought by Christ's death and resurrection.

Clarence Jordan eschewed the political marches and protest demonstrations of the era, believing instead that the most effective means to make a difference in society was to bear witness to the difference Christ had made in the world. That is, by living, in community, the radically different life made possible by God raising Jesus from the dead. Hewing to the model of the church laid out in the New Testament, therefore, the Koinonia Farm committed to embodying in its midst equality of all persons, rejection of violence, stewardship of the land, and common ownership of all money and material possessions. For the first few years, the Christians at Koinonia Farm amounted to little more than a curiosity to its neighbors in Sumter County, Georgia.

As the Civil Rights Movement began in earnest, however, the white residents of Americus, Georgia increasingly viewed the Koinonia Farm with suspicion and, later, as a threat. By the early 1960s, segregationists—so-called Christians—targeted Koinonia with economic boycotts, violence, vandalism, and, eventually, bombings. One winter, during the early 1960s, the local heating oil company began boycotting the Koinonia Farm.

Worried the residents of the farm would freeze to death, Clarence Jordan approached his brother Robert, a big-shot attorney in Atlanta, to represent the Christian community in suing the company. Robert Jordan would later become a state senator and State Supreme Court Justice.

As the theologian James McClendon recounts in his book, *Biography as Theology*, Robert Jordan responded to his brother's request by saying,

> "Clarence, I can't do that. You know my political aspirations. Why, if I represented you, I might lose my job, my house, everything I've got.... I follow Jesus, Clarence, up to a point."
>
> "Could that point, Bob, by any chance be—the cross?"
>
> "That's right. I follow Jesus to the cross, but not *on* the cross. I'm not getting myself crucified."
>
> "Then I don't believe you're a disciple. You're an admirer of Jesus, but not a disciple of his. I think you ought to go back to the church where you belong to, and tell them you're an admirer not a disciple."
>
> "Well now, if everyone who felt like I do did that, we wouldn't *have* a church, would we?"
>
> "The question," Clarence said, "is, 'Do you have a church?'"[1]

Do you have a church? Or do you have a club? Are you a church? Or are you the Jesus Admiration Society? Are you followers of Christ? Or are you the Jesus Memorial Society?

Paul has spilled so much ink writing to the Galatians about forgiveness of sins and freedom from the law that the notion of following Christ might seem to us like a non sequitur.

Indeed, what the apostle Paul says about justification in Christ alone, by grace alone, through faith alone, particularly in the Letter to the Galatians, has been so consequential for the Protestant message it's easy to fail to attend to what Paul goes on to write in the remainder of his Epistle. This is the pivot in Paul's argument, the point at which the apostle transitions from the forgiveness that is ours through faith to the end for which that forgiveness is graciously given, namely, the freedom to live as a pilgrim people.

It follows then that the gospel is about more than the forgiveness of sins. Rather, the forgiveness of sins is the necessary condition for the freedom to discover the fullness of salvation made possible by the fact the Crucified Christ is the Living LORD. For so long as you are alienated from God and neighbor by your sin, you are unavailable to be God's resident aliens in the world.

1. McClendon, *Biography as Theology*, 89.

The gospel is about more than the forgiveness of sins. The gospel is about our being made citizens of a time and space that is in tension with all other forms of citizenship. Faith alone—*sola fides*—justifies, Paul has told us in his letter. Our justification, our enough-ness before God, is nothing else than believing God when God makes a promise. Faith, Paul has insisted, the unwavering and steadfast reliance on God's promise, is what makes us righteous, not the works of the law. After all, Paul has already pointed out to the Galatians that Abraham believed God hundreds of years before God even gave the law.

And as with Abraham so it is with us. Our faith in the promise of God is reckoned to us as righteousness. The doctrine of justification by faith is at the heart of the Protestant Reformation and thus, as Stanley Hauerwas says, it should at the heart of our Protestant hearts.[2]

The only problem with the doctrine of justification so understood, however, is that the promise God makes does not stop with—and therefore it is not reducible to—the promise, "Your sins are forgiven." We're accustomed to asking the question, "Why was Jesus crucified?" Less often do we attend to the question, "Why was Paul executed?" To ask why Rome executed Paul for preaching the gospel is to posit a correlative question, "Why were the first Christians willing to die for the gospel?" The forgiveness of sins does not seem to be a message about which Caesar would find it necessary to make martyrs. No doubt you think it's good news that in Jesus Christ your sins are forgiven, but the empire seems unlikely to notice, much less care. To account for the fact of Paul's own death, to account for the fact that so many of the first Christians gave their own lives for the sake of the gospel, we can only conclude that the gospel is about more than forgiveness and that when Paul speaks of our "citizenship in heaven" it's more than a metaphor.

The gospel is bigger than the forgiveness of sins. The forgiveness of sins is not an end in itself. The forgiveness of sins is instrumental. The forgiveness of sins sets us free to be his peculiar people in the world. The formation of such a people, after all, is precisely the promise God makes to Abraham.

It's true, as Paul points out, Abraham believed God and God reckoned his faith to him as righteousness; however, who Abraham believed is inextricable from what Abraham believed. Paul simply assumes you know the content of the promise God promises to Abraham. Abraham believed

2. Hauerwas, *Minding the Web*, 200.

God's promise that through Abraham God would bring into being—create from the nothingness of Sarah's barren womb—a particular people through whom God would heal his sin-scarred world. Or, to render it according to Paul's allegory, Abraham believed God when God promised that through Abraham God would call into existence a people who would live in the world but not of the world, a people who would live on earth as it is in heaven—in the Jerusalem below but in allegiance to the Jerusalem that is above—a people who would have no Caesar but the King whose throne is a cross, a people who, by so doing, might bear witness to the truth that those who carry crosses, and not those who build them, are working with the grain of the universe.

When Robert Jordan resisted his brother's plea for him to represent the Koinonia Farm in court, Clarence Jordan pointed out that his brother wasn't the only one who risked suffering great cost.

> "*We* might lose everything too, Bob."
> "It's different for you."
> "Why is it different? I remember, it seems to me, that you and I joined the church the same Sunday, as boys. I expect when we came forward the preacher asked me about the same question he did you. He asked me, 'Do you accept Jesus as your Lord and Savior?' And I said, 'Yes.' What did you say?"[3]

The distinction drawn by Clarence Jordan between admirer and follower is a contrast in citizenship. In order to succeed as a citizen of America, particularly the America of the Jim Crow South, Robert Jordan balked at living into what his brother Clarence deemed a more determinative citizenship, namely, his citizenship in heaven. "Give to Caesar what is Caesar's. Give to God what is God's," is our usual solution to this quandary. The trouble is Caesar wants it all. Moreover, what belongs to God? Everything. Jesus doesn't want your heart. He says so to Nicodemus. He's after the whole world he so loved.

The political philosopher Jean-Jacques Rousseau, whom you may recall from your high school American history class and whose 1762 book *The Social Contract* informed the Founding Fathers, warned that the universal nature of the church posed the greatest threat to the legitimacy of the nation-state, precisely because the head of the church, Jesus Christ, is every bit as imperial in his claims over us as the state is. Rousseau went so far in his admonition about the dangers of the church as to call the term "Christian

---

3. McClendon, *Biography as Theology*, 95.

citizen"[4] an oxymoron. Rousseau, who was decidedly not a Christian, saw a tension in Christianity that many Christians no longer see. That Rousseau was a decisive influence on the Founding Fathers should leave us to wonder just who the separation of church and state is meant to protect, and it should leave little wonder that only in America will you hear Christians utter a self-negating statement like, "I believe Jesus Christ is LORD, but that's just my personal opinion." So long as our faith is relegated to a private affection of the heart, to a matter of personal choice and subjective belief, then Jesus is necessarily demoted from LORD to Secretary of Afterlife Affairs. And that's no small problem for, as Paul argues in our text today, God has invaded our world in Jesus Christ to set us free to live as the offspring of Sarah rather than of Hagar. To live, Paul writes, as children of the Jerusalem that is above. To live, that is, as citizens of heaven.

In order to appreciate how the churches in Galatia would have heard our text today about living in allegiance to the city of God, I think it important to understand what they would have seen everyday in the cities of Galatia. The historian Tom Holland, in his recent book *Dominion: How the Christian Revolution Remade the World*, writes, "To visit the cities of Galatia was to be reminded of the scale of Augustus Caesar's achievements."[5] At the center of the triple-arched gateway into Galatia stood a massive statue of Augustus on horseback. The statue was labeled, *Divii Filius*.

The Son of God.

Five years after Augustus Caesar died, it was decreed that a bronzed inscription of Augustus's career be mounted on buildings and monuments all over Galatia. Augustus himself had written the inscription. He called it the *Euangelion*—from which we get the word "evangelical." The good news. This gospel reads as follows: "He brings war to an end; he orders peace; by manifesting himself, he surpasses the hopes of all who were looking for good news." This gospel was inscribed on nearly everything all over the cities of Galatia, just as "Caesar Augustus, Son of God" was etched into every Roman coin in every Galatian pocket.

Paul's gospel was bound to raise eyebrows, Holland observes, for the Son of God (neither the one who lived in Rome nor the one who had died in Jerusalem) did not share sovereignty.

Holland writes,

---

4. Rousseau, *Social Contract*, 270.

5. Holland, *Dominion*, 81.

> To abandon the cult of the Caesars was therefore not merely to court danger, but to risk the very stitching that held together the patchwork society of Galatia's cities . . . for to repudiate the confession "Caesar is LORD" was to repudiate as well the rhythms of civic life. It was to imperil relations with family and friends. It was to show disrespect to the empire and all who served it and sacrificed for it. It was to live at home as though in exile, as a pilgrim people no longer at ease in the very land in which they lived.[6]

You have to understand, Holland points out, so extreme was the sense of dislocation experienced by converts to Paul's gospel that some of them were desperate for an old, familiar way of belonging in the world; so much so that grown men countenanced circumcision.

The false teachers' message in Galatia, adding the law back onto the gospel, was appealing exactly to the extent it offered Christians a way to go on living as though there had not been "a convulsive upheaval in the affairs of heaven and earth."[7] The appeal of the false teachers' glawspel message: it wasn't simply about trying to earn God's redemption; it was about trying to remain within the familiar parameters of the old age. In other words—think about it—it's easier to get by in the empire by going under the mohel's knife than by refusing to take up the sword. It's easier to get by in the kingdoms of this world by keeping kosher than by pledging an allegiance to Christ the King.

A dozen years ago, in my previous congregation, a worshipper about my age came up to me in the fellowship hall after the early service. He shook my hand and said, "We just wanted you to know this will be our last Sunday here."

Great, I thought, *what did I do this time to offend people?*

"Last Sunday? But why?"

"We're moving—back to Michigan. I quit my job. I'm going to go back and teach at my university instead."

Mark and his wife, veterans of Young Life and InterVarsity, had volunteered in our youth program, and so I knew both of them a little. She was a musician, and Mark, I knew, was a nuclear physicist, an honest-to-goodness rocket scientist with a well-paid job with a defense contractor.

"Why'd you quit your job?" I asked.

---

6. Holland, *Dominion*, 83.

7. Holland, *Dominion*, 87.

And he gestured to me with his coffee cup like I was complicit in some way.

"Ever since I finished my postgraduate studies," he said, "I've been making bombs. I concluded one Sunday, about six months ago, that I couldn't continue doing what I was doing and still call myself a follower of Christ. Actually, you were the preacher that day."

And I took a step back from him and stammered a little. Honestly, I felt embarrassed. I mean, I'm a United Methodist pastor. We don't often encounter people who take Jesus so seriously.

"Don't worry," he said, "I'm not saying you're responsible. I don't even remember your sermon that Sunday."

"Well, how'd you make a decision like that?"

He looked like he'd already thought about it and knew the answer.

"It feels like the decision was sort of made for me."

"Your wife?"

"No, it was in worship," he said. "I was standing there and saying the creed like we do every single Sunday. But that Sunday I said the line, 'I believe in Jesus Christ, his only Son our LORD . . .' and all of sudden it just sort of struck me that that's like a pledge of allegiance to Jesus. And, before we'd even finished the creed, I thought to myself, 'Well, how can I pledge allegiance to him here on Sunday and then on Monday morning . . . ?'"

His voice trailed off, and I didn't need him to complete his sentence. Then he started a new one.

"I've recited the creed probably every Sunday for my whole life. Maybe it's crazy, but it feels like God was using it that whole time to bring me to now."

"Sounds like it was a pretty easy decision for you then," I said.

He shook his head.

"Easy? No, it's not been easy at all," he said. "My Dad said I'd become a religious zealot and that he was ashamed of me for making my decision. My brother accused me of betraying my country and won't talk to me."

"I'm so sorry," I said, secretly glad to steer our conversation toward less threatening, pastoral territory.

"Sorry?" he said, like he was genuinely surprised by response. "Why are you sorry? Who ever said following Jesus was supposed to be easy?"

In 1940, after the fall of France, Jewish refugees began arriving by the hundreds at the Protestant village of Le Chambon-sur-Lignon. Many of the refugees were children. Without so much as a discussion or debate, the village pastor, André Trocmé, and his parishioners began taking the refugees into their homes and barns and, whenever German soldiers showed up, hiding the refugees up in the mountains. Still more refugees arrived as word among the Jews spread that this was a community whose only Führer was Jesus Christ.

Here's the thing. The villagers of Le Chambon never decided that their home would become a haven for refugees. They never held a vote. They never convened a city council or scheduled a church meeting. Neither the pastor nor anyone else in the community of Christians suggested that this was their cross to bear. In the process of following Jesus Christ, they simply now found themselves with refugees in their homes.

Once, in February 1943, Nazi police arrived to arrest the pastor and some of his parishioners. The police officers sat in a villager's living room waiting for the would-be prisoners to go fetch their suitcases. The woman in whose house they waited invited the policemen to join her at her dinner table—despite the fact that Jews were hiding upstairs in her bedroom. When asked how she could be so hospitable to enemies who were there to take her husband away, perhaps to his death, the woman, Magda, replied: "It was dinner time . . . the food was ready . . . how could I not invite them to eat with me? Don't use such foolish words as 'forgiving' and 'good' with me. Inviting strangers and enemies to supper is just the normal thing to do if Jesus is LORD."[8]

Villagers later told a biographer they did not believe their actions were heroic. In fact, they did not believe they were even ultimately responsible for their actions. "All this time," one woman explained, "Christ had been forming us—hearing his Word, praying his prayer, receiving his body and blood—to be his people for this time, here in this place. What else could we do?"[9]

"I think you ought to go back to the church where you belong," Clarence Jordan told his brother, Robert, "let them know you're not really a follower of Jesus, you're an admirer."[10]

Most of us are admirers of Jesus. Thank God, then, that being Christ's followers is gospel, not law. It's a promise. "I will be your God," the LORD promises. "And you will be my people" (Jer 30:22). Most of us—certainly myself included—are only admirers of Jesus. Yet the promise is that Christ

<hr>

8. Hallie, *Lest Innocent Blood Be Shed,* 171.

9. Hallie, *Lest Innocent Blood Be Shed,* 273.

10. McClendon, *Biography as Theology,* 89.

Jesus has redeemed us to be so much more than we would be. And because Jesus is not dead, we should expect to be made more than we would otherwise dare. You see, it's not just our forgiveness that we must take on faith alone. We've got to take it on faith that God is using means as mundane as bread and wine—and words—to make us into a people capable of working with the grain of the universe.

Walking into Speech

Galatians 5:1–6, 13–15

T WO STORIES:

Shane Clifton is a professor of theology at Alphacrucis College in Australia. In October 2010, Clifton suffered an injury while jumping a bicycle, an event he describes matter-of-factly as "a contingent event that is part and parcel for what it means to be a creature of the earth." Such a matter-of-fact description is, in fact, quite terrifying, for Clifton's everyday bicycle accident rendered him a complete (C5) quadripalegic. His memoir, *Husbands Should Not Break,* is a book in which the author resists writing what he elsewhere calls "inspiration porn."[1]

Clifton speaks candidly about the depression and despair that attended his seven-month rehabilitation in Prince of Wales Hospital in Sydney and the dark night of the soul that soon followed. About the time immediately after his discharge, Clifton writes:

> Eventually I arrived home, and entered a house bedecked with balloons and streamers, to the cheers and tears of my wife and children. We were all excited but, although we didn't voice our concerns, we were also a little nervous—like newlyweds on a honeymoon, in love, but tentative. Not long after I arrived, Elly looked my way, smiled, and wrapped her arms around my shoulders. Looking on, the boys joined in spontaneously, a five-person hug that expressed our love and constrained our fear. There was one problem. I had forgotten to turn my wheelchair's power off, and with Jacob accidentally leaning against my joystick, we were propelled like a rugby scrum into the kitchen table, which in turn smashed through our rear window, spraying shards of glass in every direction. It put an end to our cuddle, but did give us something to laugh about. What we didn't realize at the time was that this event would turn out to be symbolic.[2]

1. Clifton, *Crippled Grace,* 15.
2. Clifton, *Crippled Grace,* 13.

To be sure, *Husbands Should Not Break* tells a harrowing story, yet it also tells a surprising story. It does not tell a story of Shane Clifton negotiating a life of challenge and struggle but nevertheless finding something approximating happiness. It instead tells a story of how Shane and his wife eventually find a deeper and more abiding happiness than the happiness that had constituted their life prior to paralysis.

Under the conditions of his new, changed life, Clifton discovered a happiness he had not previously known, a happiness that is discovered not in spite of his struggles but because of them. To be disabled, Clifton writes, is to be in a near constant state of sheer vulnerability before others and absolute dependency upon God and neighbor. Such dependency usually strikes us as an ordeal to be avoided at all costs, but, through it, Clifton received a life he would not trade for any other life.

"Paralysis liberated me," he says.[3]

That's the first story. The second story you might've seen in the news. Irwin Bernstein, a retired Air Force veteran, was recently serving a second, postretirement stint on the faculty at the University of Georgia. When the fall semester began last week, Professor Bernstein made clear to the students enrolled in his psychology class that he would not make any exceptions to his mandatory mask policy.

"No mask, no class," the professor wrote on the white board on the first day before handing out the syllabus.[4] Bernstein explained to the class that he had come out of retirement to teach them and that, because of his old age and underlying medical condition, he expected his students to respect his rule. He suffers type two diabetes and high blood pressure, and contracting the coronavirus could very easily be lethal to him. If anyone suspected that perhaps the professor of psychology was conducting his own real-time psychological test, those suspicions were dashed by the next class.

On the second day of class, a student, Hannah Huff, defiantly showed up without a mask.

When handed a mask by a classmate, the student put it on but refused to wear it over her nose. When Professor Bernstein asked her repeatedly to wear the mask properly, she ignored him, pretending not to hear him. Finally, Bernstein stopped pleading with her and announced to his seminar students that he was resigning.

3. Clifton, *Crippled Grace,* 16.
4. Steinbuch, "Professor Resigns," para. 6.

On the spot. He gathered up his briefcase and books and walked out of the classroom. Later, the professor told the campus newspaper that whereas he had risked his life to defend his country while in the Air Force, he was not willing to risk his life to teach a class with an unmasked student during this pandemic. Professor Bernstein, who's nearly ninety years old, says he's received many, many messages due to his decision to retire, with some expressing support for his decision but many others expressing anger and using profane language over the way the professor impinged on the "liberty" of his student.

When asked about her refusal to wear a mask, Hannah replied with pride that she can do what she wants. If she doesn't want to wear a mask, she should not have to wear a mask. It's a matter freedom, she insisted.

I begin with these two stories about freedom because one of these stories is about what Christians mean by the word "freedom" and the other of these stories is about the opposite of what Christians mean by "freedom." The contrast between these two stories reminds us, therefore, that, as much as it is anything else, Christianity is a language, and to be a Christian is, in no small measure, to work with words that possess particular meanings, meanings that are determined by the Word who was made flesh.

In other words, what we talk about when we talk about the word freedom is not necessarily—or rather, is necessarily not—what others talk about when they talk about freedom. In writing about language and the training that language requires, the philosopher Stanley Cavell recalls a memory from his daughter's childhood. From an illustration in one of her very first board books as a toddler, Cavell's daughter learned to say the word "kitty." She pointed to the bright and simple illustration of a cat in her baby book and she sounded out the word "kitty." Some weeks later, however, the little girl came across a fur coat—a mink—stroked it, and said the word "kitty," making Cavell realize that his daughter really did not know what the word "kitty" means.[5]

The word "kitty" had a more specific definition than his daughter yet understood. Only when she gets to pet a litter of kittens, to watch them bob and chase after a tiny ball or to feel them climb on her lap and up her chest or to hear their deep purring, will she learn the word's true meaning. Only then, Cavell suggests, will she "walk into speech."[6]

5. Hauerwas, *Fully Alive*, 28.
6. Cavell, *Claim of Reason*, 169.

What is the speech into which Paul would have us walk when it comes to the peculiar, counterintuitive way he uses this word "freedom?"

"The Anointed freed us for freedom."

The apostle Paul writes today at the climax of his Letter to the Galatians, "stand fast, then, and do not again be restrained by slavery's yoke . . . for you were called to freedom, brothers [and sisters]; only let this freedom not serve as an occasion for the flesh; rather slave for one another by love. For the whole law is summed up in a single utterance; to wit: 'You shall love your neighbor as yourself'" (Matt 22:37–39).

Hang on. Paul has spent four angry, polemical chapters declaring his opponents anathema for attempting to add the law back onto the gospel. To add to the gospel is to subtract the whole gospel. Christ plus anything else at all is no gospel at all. To make our works necessary to the gospel is to nullify the work of Christ. Any false teacher who makes circumcision a condition for acceptance by God should go all the way, Paul indelicately put it, and castrate themselves. By the law I died to the law, for if justification comes through the law, then Christ died for absolutely nothing, Paul wrote in chapter 2. Your justification, your enough-ness before God comes not through obedience to the law, Paul has repeated over and over and over; it comes through faith *sola*, alone. You are justified—only—in Christ alone by grace alone through faith alone.

But now, having dispensed with all his talk of justification, it sounds like Paul is committing the worst and most common mistake preachers make—that is, taking away with one hand the free grace the preacher has given with the other hand. It sounds like Paul is doing exactly what the false teachers do, muddling the law with the gospel, adding *do* to the message of *done*, confusing commands with promise, attaching our work to God's gift. It sounds like Paul is saying here that Christ has set us free for exactly what Paul previously told us that Christ has set us free from, namely, a life lived in obedience to the law. "Christ has set you free to slave for one another by love," and the word Paul uses there in conjunction with the word freedom is, in fact, the word for "slave," *doulos*, as though gospel freedom is a form of slavery to God's law. "For the whole law is summed up in a single utterance," Paul writes; "to wit: 'You shall love your neighbor as yourself.'"

Evidently, we have not been set free by Christ to do whatever we want.

Christ has set us free to be slaves to the wants of God.

Notice, if gospel freedom is a form of slavery to God's law, then when Paul today warns us not to submit again to the yoke of a different form of slavery, the slavery he has in mind is what we most often understand in America as freedom. In other words, if true freedom is slavery to the law of God, then true slavery is the "freedom" to be our own law. If genuine freedom looks like bondage to the wants of God, then actual bondage looks like freedom to do whatever we want.

Paraphrasing St. Paul's paradoxical understanding of Christian liberty, Martin Luther famously says in his treatise *On the Freedom of a Christian*, "A Christian is a perfectly free LORD of all, subject to none. A Christian is a perfectly dutiful slave of all, subject to all."[7] Not only is this a peculiar way to define a word like freedom, it's a definition of freedom that we cannot understand apart from remembering the fact that, out of all the peoples of the world, God has called the Jews to be his particular people. That is, when the apostle Paul announces, "For freedom, Christ has set us free," the speech Paul would have us walk into—and be schooled by—is the grammar of the only Scriptures Paul knew: our Old Testament.

I took a Jewish Studies course as a undergraduate at the University of Virginia, and I recall how in one class, during a discussion of the Torah, the professor, Dr. Peter Ochs, joked that, "Any religion that doesn't tell you what to do with your pots and your pans and your genitals isn't a religion worth following." All of us in the class laughed at his joke, despite the fact that none of us knew what he meant by it. Finally, one brave student raised her hand and said, "I don't get it." And Dr. Ochs smiled and said, "Any religion that doesn't tell you what to do with your pots and your pans and your genitals lacks a god who is determined to make you fully free."

When Paul uses a word like "freedom," the speech Paul would have us enter is the language of the exodus. Seldom do we notice, but when God gives the law to the Israelites at Mount Sinai he does so in order to set them free from captivity to false gods. The commands of the covenant are a means of liberation. I recently watched the scene as depicted in Cecile B. DeMille's film version starring Charleston Heston, and I was surprised by the movie's accuracy to the text. When Moses strides down the mountain only to discover the Israelites have stooped to worshipping a golden calf, Moses bellows at them, "You are not worthy to receive these ten commandments!"

"We will not live by your commandments, we're free!" someone in the crowd shouts.

7. Luther, *Freedom of a Christian*, 18.

"There is no freedom without the law!" Moses replies, pointing to the stone tablets in his hands.[8]

God's people, Scripture says, are free because they live under God's law. The commands of the law are not the limits God sets around his people's freedom. The commands of the covenant, right down to every jot and tittle about pots and pans and genitals—commands that can be encapsulated, Paul says today, in the command to love our neighbors as ourselves—are the way God sets his people free.

Free from what?

How does God telling us what to do constitute freedom?

The late Catholic theologian Herbert McCabe argues in *Law, Love, and Language* that all ten commandments of the Decalogue—as well as the hundreds of other laws of the Mosaic covenant—are meant to reiterate the first commandment, "I am the LORD your God, who brought you out of the land of Egypt, out of the house of slavery; you shall have no God but YHWH, the God who sets you free." Thus, the law, McCabe says, is actually a charter of liberation. The commandments are ways we learn to live not as slaves to the false gods—and very often we're our own false gods—but as subjects of the True and Living LORD. McCabe observes how of all the animals God has made we are the only animals in creation who know not how to be creatures. Thus, to be free is to be schooled in the vulnerability, contingency, and dependence that constitutes creaturehood.

That God tells us what to do with our bodies, for example, is a reminder that we are not gods; therefore, the bodies of others are not objects to which we're entitled. That God tells us what to do with our pots and our pans is a reminder that, though it's true that "one does not live by bread alone," it's just as surely true that one cannot live without bread, bread the mercy of our Maker alone provides. That God commands us not to kill and to love our neighbor as ourself, even the neighbor who is also our enemy, is a reminder that we are but creatures and that this is the form our Creator's care of us took when he took flesh.

To assert, as St. Paul has in his Letter to the Galatians, that the purpose of the law is not to justify you is not to suggest that the law has no purpose.

The purpose of the law is to teach you how to be a creature.

It's not about being justified, it's about becoming human. As fully human as, say, Shane Clifton. In his memoir, *Husbands Should Not Break*, Shane Clifton writes,

8. DeMille, *Ten Commandments*, 1:26–1:29.

In an instant, I was made one whom others, when hearing about such a life, say, "They'd be better off dead," and tell their own loved ones, "If that ever happens to me, unplug the machine," but the paradox of paralysis, being rendered completely vulnerable and totally dependent and constantly aware of the contingency of my creature-hood, is that I've never been more free.[9]

I thought of Clifton's book suddenly one Sunday morning. During an August worship service, an usher flagged me from the rear of the sanctuary. After the last few worshippers trickled through my communion line, I carried the body and blood of Christ to a woman to whom the usher pointed. She and her husband sat behind the back pew, he in a chair pulled from the lobby and she in her wheelchair. Living with MS, her body was tense and her movements halting. I broke off a piece of bread. Praying it wouldn't prove too large, I place it in between her clenched fingers.

"The body of Christ broken for you," I whispered.

I watched as her husband guided the host to her clenched but eager mouth. She chewed slowly as though she knew better than us that her life depended upon what lay within it. He waited calmly. I watched the clock nervously. When finally she swallowed, her husband guided the cup to her lips.

"The blood of Christ poured out for you, honey."

He'd stolen my line.

Some of the wine dribbled out of her mouth and onto her easy-snap blouse. Unwrapping the cloth from the stem of the chalice, he wiped her face clean and blotted the stain on her shirt.

"A Christian," Martin Luther says, "is a perfectly free LORD of all, subject to none. A Christian is a perfectly dutiful slave of all, subject to all."[10]

It took the better part of two verses of a hymn for Frank to serve Tina.

"I admire you," I said to him later.

"For what?"

He genuinely did not know.

"For the way you are with her," I said. "Your patience and tenderness."

"This is my life," he said, "I don't want any other."

That's freedom.

That's freedom.

That's the freedom for which Christ has set us free.

9. Clifton, *Crippled Grace*, 112.

10. Luther, *Freedom of a Christian*, 18.

We live at a time and in a culture that defines freedom the way the Bible defines sin: complete autonomy. But the word "autonomy" in Greek, *auto + nomos*, literally means to be a law unto your own self, which is as good a definition as any for godlessness. To be free, our culture tells us, is to be free from external constraints and from the claims of others. Freedom so understood is the liberty to be left alone. Freedom is the latitude to do what you, as an individual, want to do.

That Christianity is a foreign language in such a culture can be illustrated by the fact that ancient and medieval Christians always depicted hell as the realm where the unrepentant are granted the prerogative to do whatever they want to do. At such a time and in such a culture, therefore, that God has told us what to do, that God has given us something to do, is not a burden but a gift.

Grace.

My oldest son, Alexander, left last summer for his freshman year at William and Mary. He was starting college with a semester abroad in Costa Rica. His flight left early that Wednesday just past midnight, so we were at Dulles late Tuesday night to see him off. I was expecting to cry. I was not expecting to cry because of the rows upon rows of Red Cross cots I saw set up throughout the terminal and the huddled groups of Afghan refugees holding frightened children and plastic bags of belongings.

Having checked his luggage, we left the ticketing desk. Walking with Alexander towards the security checkpoint, I bumped into a young woman exiting a restroom. She was wearing a soft pink hijab and held an impossibly tiny baby across her chest. Both of them, baby and mother, had dirt and blood on their clothes and cheeks. I bumped into her and, in an instant, a news story, from which I had heretofore been comfortably removed, collided into me.

"I'm sorry. Excuse me," I said, hoping to avoid tearing up in front of her. As I helped her pick up belongings, I thought of the law, "Welcome the refugee among you and care for them, for once you were a refugee in the land of Egypt."

Bumping into her, it was like walking into speech.

To be so reminded of my obligation to someone like her, it wasn't a burden. It was a gift. I left the airport that night more what God made me to be.

That's freedom.

That's freedom.

But to so understand freedom is to speak a strange and difficult language in a foreign culture whose words often mean otherwise. Fortunately, Christ has given us the bread and wine that is his body and blood. Christ has given us neighbors and possibly even enemies. Christ has given us the poor, whom we always will have with us, so that, for a world in need of witnesses, we might learn to walk into this speech.

Verification Principle

Galatians 5:16–26

I N THE MIDDLE AGES, the Benedictine monastery in the town of Cluny, in the Burgundy region of France, implemented a modest civic policy that soon made its way across the feudal communities of western Europe and was practiced, in some fashion or another, for nearly 500 years. The Benedictines called their arrangement the "Peace of God" or "the Truce of God." The Peace of God measure mandated the suspension of all warfare during certain days of the week, as well as high holy days and liturgical seasons.

Initially, the Truce of God stipulated the cessation of all violence from Saturday night until dusk on Monday. Soon after, the Truce extended the law to lay down arms from Wednesday night through Monday morning of every week. The experiment known as the "Peace of God" grew out of the Benedictines' recognition that the lordship of the Crucified Jesus, which Christians professed on Sunday, carried with it practical implications for how Christians lived Monday through Saturday.

Indeed, that feudal lords accepted the premise behind the Truce of God, however reluctantly or imperfectly they did so, shows their acknowledgment that how Christians live Monday through Saturday risks invalidating the truth claims they make on Sunday. Of course, the Decalogue forbids God's people from the killing of anyone, but even in the Middle Ages Christians realized their willingness to wreak violence upon other Christians rendered their worship of the Prince of Peace unintelligible. That is, it falsified their faith, for if the gospel is nothing other than news, then the gospel cannot be known apart from witnesses—witnesses, moreover, whose lives exemplify the truth of that news.

Stanley Hauerwas likes to tell the story of how he hung a poster on his office door at Duke University. The poster had been published by the Mennonite Central Committee, and, overtop an arresting image of two people in grief embracing one another, the text on the poster says, "A Modest Proposal for Peace: Let the Christians of the World Agree That They Will Not Kill Each Other." Every year for over twenty years, Stanley likes to share, students would knock on his door. Angry and offended by the poster, they'd say to Stanley, "This makes me so mad. Christians shouldn't kill anybody."

"The Mennonites called it a modest proposal," Stanley always replies. "You've got to start somewhere."

On the theory that you've got to start somewhere, in the Middle Ages, the Benedictines took the practical step of banning warfare and violence from sundown on Wednesday to sunup on Monday. If Christians were going to disobey their LORD and contradict the baptismal covenant they were now limited to three days a week in which to do it. The Peace of God in the eleventh century included an oath in which the Christian swore:

> I will not attack a villain or villainess or servants or merchants for ransom. I will not take a mule or a horse male or female or a colt in pasture from any man from the month of March to the feast of the All Saints unless to recover a debt. I will not attack noble ladies traveling without husband nor their maids, nor widows or nuns unless it is their fault. From the beginning of Lent to the end of Easter I will not attack an unarmed knight.[1]

Just imagine the oath if the Benedictines had had to account for the people in their parish using Facebook or Twitter. Medieval Christians seem very odd to most of us today; nevertheless, they had a certain instinctive sense that worship was not a matter simply of belief, but both declared and actualized certain policies for meaningful living. Rather than rationalize and self-justify why our Monday through Saturday commitments do not comport with our Sunday morning claim that Jesus is LORD, Rowan Williams says, it would be better to renounce our faith altogether and sin boldly.[2] For when we separate our faith from our witness, we separate Christ's work from Christ's person. And when we separate the work of Christ from the person of Christ—when we separate the message about Jesus from the message of Jesus—we make the church invisible in the world.

That is, if what it means to be a Christian is a belief in your head or a feeling in your heart, then Christians no longer offer the world lives that are an exemplification of the kingdom we await. Or, to put it in the terms with which Paul writes in his Letter to the Galatians, when we separate our faith and our witness, the person of Christ and the work of Christ, the

---

1. Williams, *Truce of God*, 10.
2. Williams, *Truce of God*, 75.

message *about* Jesus from the message *of* Jesus, we forget that the result of the Holy Spirit resting upon us in the gift of faith is the same result as when the Holy Spirit overshadowed Mary.

Incarnation.

When the Holy Spirit rests upon us at baptism, the result is the same as when the Holy Spirit rested upon Mary. The result is Christ. In both cases, the Holy Spirit conceives Christ. The fruit of the Spirit is God made flesh in the world. "But the fruit of the Spirit is love, joy, peace, patience, kindness, goodness, faithfulness, gentleness, self-mastery; against such things there is no law." To turn the fruit of the Spirit into a list of *oughts* or advice—a good Christian *should* be kind—assumes that we bring to such virtues definitions that are already more or less correct. It assumes we naturally know what love is, say, or patience or self-control, and that we know how to practice them. But that is certainly not how the apostle Paul thinks of them. That Paul uses the language of the Spirit's fruit means these attributes are gifts, gifts that come through the training of the whole church—training Paul calls "crucifying the flesh."

The very language of crucifixion, moreover, is a clue that the fruit of the Spirit is not even primarily a description of us.

When it comes to requests to preside at weddings, I say "No" more often than I say "Yes." Even when I do capitulate, it's with the condition that the couple not ask me to preach on 1 Corinthians 13.

"The Bible's obviously not much interested in marriage, certainly not in married love," I tell them, "but that's no excuse to turn Paul's letter into something it's not."

"Faith, hope and love abide, but love never ends . . ."

For Paul, only Jesus, who was before creation and who was raised from the dead, is without beginning and end.

"Paul's talking about Jesus," I tell brides and grooms. "Jesus is patient, Jesus is kind, Jesus is not envious or boastful or arrogant or rude. Jesus does not insist on his own way."

Paul's describing Jesus, not us. Likewise, in this section of Galatians he's talking about Jesus. The virtues Paul lists are firstly a description of Jesus, and, therefore, they derive their definitions from the narratives of his life. It's from Jesus, who so refuses to save us through violence that he suffers our violence, that we learn the meanings of faithfulness, self-control, and love. It's from Jesus, who commands us to confront the brother or sister who has sinned against us, if necessary involving the whole community of disciples, that we learn that peace is neither easy work nor can it be confused for sentimentality. We learn kindness from the one who forgives three times the Peter who had thrice denied him. We learn joy from the one who makes the best wine for a party too drunk to appreciate it. We learn the nature of gentleness from the one who refuses to cast the first stone but nonetheless rightly names the woman's sin as sin. By breaking the law in order to eat and drink with sinners, Jesus gives us a definition of goodness we could not have apart from Jesus.

Paul's talking about Jesus.

Jesus is the one whose cross and resurrection have graced us with this in-between time, between the old age and the new one, so that we might have all the time in the world to shape our lives according to his kingdom. That's patience. That's God's patience.

The fruits of the Spirit describe Christ.

But do not forget: the Christ born to Mary is not the only Christ made flesh in the world. There is also the body that is Christ, born not to Mary but of water and the Spirit. That is, the church. Just as the Holy Spirit anoints Mary's son and sends him out into the world to confront the world with an alternative to the world, so too does the Holy Spirit anoint and send Christ's body into the world to bear witness to a kingdom whose virtues are intelligible only in the light of Easter. In other words, the fruits of the Spirit are not attributes to which any individual should aspire, nor are they a code of conduct individual Christians ought to obey. They describe the body of Christ that the Holy Spirit makes flesh for the world.

Paul could be writing to Nicodemus instead of sending this letter to the Galatians. "For God so loved the world, he gave it his body," Paul could say, "the church." Indeed Christ's body is even less impressive and more counter-intuitive than the body of a Jewish carpenter from Nazareth. Nevertheless, it's a body through whose life—a particular life marked by love, joy, peace, patience, kindness, goodness, faithfulness, gentleness, and self-control—the world might know it's the world. That is, through Christ's body the world might know it's a good gift cared for by a gracious God. This is why Paul views it as a profound mistake that the false teachers would add the law back onto the gospel—because the Holy Spirit is already doing what the law originally envisaged. The Holy Spirit is making flesh a people, a peculiar people, a witnessing minority, who might be a light to the nations.

I remember, twenty years ago, I was working in the mailroom at Princeton before my late-morning class. My supervisor, Vince, was on the phone with his wife, who was in the hospital dying of cancer. She told him to find a television and then, he said, the line went dead. The nearest TV that September 11 was mounted in the corner outside the dining hall. The TV was on mute. And for a while all of us standing there, staring up at the buildings, we were on mute too. Until the first tower fell and the silence became a chorus of whispered "Oh my Gods."

The first time I preached was the sermon for the following Sunday.

I'd just been appointed by a bishop who was desperate to fill a vacancy at a small, clergy-killing church and who had scoured the seminary for a United Methodist student. I made the mistake of trying to say too much in my sermon that Sunday, as though God needed defending.

Fred was a quiet, elderly African American who served as the patriarch of the congregation. I didn't know it at the time. Fred's son always attended service with his Father, but Fred sat alone that Sunday after the eleventh and every Sunday thereafter. His son's office had been in the second tower.

I remember, just a few weeks later, I was making my way from a coffee shop to campus and I stumbled upon Fred standing in a crowd on Nassau Square. Fred was wearing a large wooden cross around his neck and was holding a sign that had a wooden paint-stirrer taped to the back. The sign was sky blue and in a bold white font it read, "Christians Against War."

"I didn't peg you for the protesting type," I said to him.

And he looked at me with an intensity that unnerved me.

"My only hope for my boy," he said, "is the resurrection. I'm clinging to the news that Jesus is alive and will put my boy back together and raise him up—and me too." I looked around at the demonstration, wondering how what he said explained what he was doing. "I saw the notice for this gathering, and I figured, if I'm counting on it being true that Jesus is LORD, then I ought to try to live like I actually believe it."

What virtue is that exactly, I wonder?

Faithfulness? Peace? Self-control?

Whatever virtue the Spirit produced in Fred, I don't have it. Likely neither do most of us. Fortunately, Paul's letter is not written just to us. It's written to the whole church. Indeed, this is why Paul uses the odd locution "the fruit of the Spirit is . . ." Paul doesn't say "the fruit of the Spirit are . . ." It's singular, "the fruit of the Spirit is . . ." That the fruit of the Spirit is singular means one virtue is not present except where all of them are present. Peace is not present apart from patience, nor faithfulness apart from self-control. Joy is not possible in the absence of goodness. And love that is not schooled by the ability to confront untruthfulness with gentleness is not love but sentimentality.

The fruit of the Spirit *is* . . .

It's all one gift. They go together. They require one another. The Spirit produces them all, not in every Christian believer, but throughout Christ's body. Which is to say, there is no way for Christians to make the gospel intelligible to the world without depending upon the lives of other Christians.

Dietrich Bonhoeffer makes the same point, commenting on the Beatitudes in Matthew's Gospel: "Each of the Beatitudes names a gift, but it is not presumed that everyone who is a follower of Jesus will possess each beatitude. Rather, the gifts so named in the Beatitudes suggest that the diversity of these gifts will be present in the community of those who have heard Jesus' call to discipleship. Indeed, to learn to be a disciple is to learn why we require one another."[3] Because none of us possess all the gifts, our lives in isolation cannot bear witness to the fullness of the kingdom.

At the beginning of his paper, "Gods," the philosopher John Wisdom tells a parable of two people who return to their garden after a long time away.[4] Rather than finding their neglected garden overgrown and desiccated, the two discover that their old plants are doing quite well.

One of the two people concludes that while they were away, a gardener must have been coming to the garden to tend the plants. But upon further investigation, they can find no evidence to suggest that the proposed gardener has been working in the garden. The one that believes there must be a gardener posits the gardener must come and work at night. The other person in the parable insists that cannot be true for surely someone at some point would have heard the gardener at work or happened upon the gardener working in the dark. The one who believes in the gardener, however, calls attention to the precise arrangement of flowers in the garden and argues that an invisible gardener must come to tend the garden. The believer believes that if they just pay closer attention to the garden, they'll confirm the necessary existence of such a gardener.

3. Bonhoeffer, *Discipleship*, 110.

4. Rutledge, *And God Spoke to Abraham*, 226.

They both study what happens when closer attention is paid to the garden but they still can reach no definitive conclusion from their empirical observation. They each see the same garden, yet one accepts the existence of a gardener and the other cannot.

Wisdom tells the parable to unpack what philosophers call the verification principle. The principle insists that all our convictions, but particularly our convictions about God, must be open to argument and investigation. The existence of a gardener is not self-evident. You can't simply assert, "I believe a gardener exists." You've got to provide an account that makes plausible your conviction that a gardener exists.

This demand for verification is even more incumbent upon Christians. After all, Christians go well beyond the general conviction that a gardener exists.

Christians make the particular claim that the gardener-with-a-capital-G is a first-century Jew from Nazareth who lived briefly, died violently, and rose unexpectedly. To claim the Gardener is the child born to Mary is a ludicrous conviction. I mean, think about it. Most people struggle simply to believe in a Gardener. To claim the Gardener is the child born to Mary is absurd on its face. There's nothing in the garden to substantiate such a claim. It requires witnesses. Witnesses whose life together substantiates the conviction that the one who preached the Sermon on the Mount is the great, cosmic Gardener.

The gospel is a self-refuting assertion apart from lives whose coherence can only be explained by the resurrection of the crucified Christ. This is what Paul means today by telling the Galatians that we not only proclaim the crucifixion, we participate in it—"crucifying the flesh."

Standing there on the town square next to Fred in October 2001, I said, "I guess I assumed you'd be consumed with anger. I'm surprised you could come out to a such a gathering."

And, I remember, he spat on the sidewalk—in disgust.

"You can't imagine the rage I feel, preacher . . ." His eyes lit up wide and then got wet. "You think I want to be here? Sure, I want to kill every last one . . ." and his voice trailed off in a string of expletives. "But if I'm depending on the LORD to give me my boy back, I can't act like the promise of resurrection is the only thing he ever said."

"The fruit of the Spirit is love, joy, peace, patience, kindness, goodness, faithfulness, gentleness, self-control . . ." No scientific investigation can posit that the gardener is Jesus. No philosophical theory can persuade that the gardener is Jesus. No historical document—certainly not the Bible—can prove that the gardener is a Jew named Jesus.

You, Christ's body, the church, are the verification principle. You are the fruit that the Spirit cultivates in the garden so that all might know not only that there is indeed a gardener but that the fullest expression of this gardener is the one who forgave his enemies while dying on a tree. In other words, our sanctification is necessary not to God but to the world. You don't need to become holy so that God can redeem you. God's already redeemed you in Jesus Christ. You need to become holy so that the world might come to recognize the character of the God who has redeemed it in a crucified savior.

If such a vocation strikes you as an extraordinary claim for ordinary people like ourselves, then take heart that the churches to whom Paul writes were even less impressive than us. That Paul admonishes them for falling back into works of the flesh is but an indication that Paul understands that the Old Adam may have been drowned in our baptisms, but that doesn't mean the Old Adam is not, as the saying goes, a mighty strong swimmer. Paul's all too aware that we remain at once sinners and saints; be that as it may, God has nevertheless called forth such imperfect people to be his particular people whose peculiar virtues might gesture toward the end all have in Christ. Looked at from God's side of this plan, it seems an odd and reckless gambit to risk so much on people like us.

Looked at from our side, it should be an occasion for joy.

In a world where life often feels like it's just one damn thing after another, God has given us—you and me!—a destiny and gifted us with something worth giving our lives to, something worth dying for.

Live Their Worst Life Now

"Bear one another's burdens, in this way you fulfill the law of Christ."

Kate Bowler is a professor at Duke Divinity School whose scholarly expertise centers on the history of the Prosperity Gospel movement in the United States. What began as a professional academic pursuit became a pressing, personal matter when Bowler, just in her mid-thirties, received a grim diagnosis of stage-four colon cancer. Recuperating from an initial surgery to remove the many lesions massed on her internal organs, Bowler shuffled Duke University Hospital's hallways still wearing her gown and tethered to an IV pole and wandering through a fog of disbelief.

In her book, *No Cure for Being Human*, she recalls how she wandered into the hospital gift shop and started to pull the books that triggered her off of the shelves. She writes:

> I can see now that it was probably alarming for the teenager at the gift shop counter to see a patient in a blue cotton gown wheel her own IV into the store, mutter loudly at a carousel of books, and begin to pull titles off the shelf. Not one by one. But dozen by dozen.
>
> "Can I help you ma'am?" the manager asks gingerly.
>
> But I am coming in hot.
>
> "Yes! Thank you. I need you to know that these books are not suitable to be sold in a hospital."
>
> I point to the pile of Christian bestsellers I've made on the floor, books that I carefully studied and documented in a comprehensive history of the movement known as the prosperity gospel. I spent ten years interviewing their celebrity authors and pulling apart their promises for divine happiness and healing with gentleness. But gentleness is not what I'm after today. The manager only stares.

"Okay, like this one for example." I nudge *Your Best Life Now* with my foot. Televangelist Joel Osteen is on the cover and leaning into the camera.

"It says here it was a *New York Times* bestseller," the manager says reasonably. "He's written about 'the prosperity gospel.' He's saying God will reward you with money and health if you have the right kind of faith."

My voice is too high, even I can hear that.

"Normally, okay. I can handle this. But you can't sell this in a hospital. You can't sell this to me."

I gesture melodramatically to my gown, and she looks away, as if to give me a moment of privacy. I gesture to another book and then another.

"This book tells me to claim my healing using Bible verses. This one tells me that if I can unleash my positive thoughts I can get rid of negativity in my life."

"So what do you recommend instead?" The manager's back is to me as she starts to reassemble the display I have dismantled. I glance around the bookstore. There are books on how to let go of the past, how to live in the present, how to claim a brighter future. I suddenly feel like I need to sit down. "Just let me point out the books that actively blame people for causing their own diseases."

Which she lets me do. The next time I wheel past the bookstore window, copies of *Your Best Life Now* have been replaced by copies of Joel Osteen's new book, *You Can, You Will*.[1]

I had my own hospital meltdown maybe six years ago.

I was sitting in the cafeteria at Johns Hopkins with a parishioner named Katherine. Her daughter was a student in my confirmation class. I'd buried her husband just three months earlier, after he'd died suddenly at home. No sooner had she put an offer on a new home where she and Beth could start fresh than Katherine started to have recurring and persistent nose bleeds. The third doctor she consulted finally discovered the tumor in her brain; at which point, her already poor odds had become a long shot.

We sat in the cafeteria. Her siblings from Scotland had taken Beth for a walk. Katherine wore a pink North Face fleece over her hospital gown. She sipped tea and wondered why she was so hungry. She'd been googling private schools on her iPhone for her daughter back home in Scotland, she told me, planning for what no longer seemed an unlikelihood. She covered

---

1. Bowler, *No Cure for Being Human*, 12–14.

her mouth as a wave of anguish crashed over her, and I could barely make out the question in her gasp.

"Why is God doing this to me?" she asked.

And then, as if to venture an answer to her question, she confessed to me mistakes in her past—an affair early in her marriage, an abortion before it—that might account for why God was afflicting her with such sorrow. Maybe it was my own pastoral exhaustion, but I smacked the cafeteria table so hard my coffee spilled across over the floor.

"God's not freaking doing this to you!" I yelled, only vaguely aware of the stares directed my way. "I've certainly got my questions about what the hell he's up to right now, but I know he's not doing this to you! God doesn't work that way."

I didn't even bother to mop up the spilled coffee.

I was angry. And I was furious not at God or the fickle cruelty of the universe. I was righteously pissed at all the many messages that muddle the gospel with the law so as to produce questions like, "Why is God doing this to me?" Because it's glawspel that produces un-Christian questions of this sort. The same assumed system of merit and demerit that says God's done his part, forgiving you all your sins in Christ Jesus, but now you've got to do your part, earning your forgiveness and accruing righteousness of your own—that same system of merit and demerit is at work in questions like "Why is God doing this to me?" The grammar of such a question depends upon the logic of the law not the gospel.

But God works by grace not law, Paul has angrily insisted for five chapters of his letter to the Galatians.

And grace is not karma.

This is why Paul adopts such a furious, four-lettered attitude in his epistle. For Paul, getting the gospel right is every bit as urgent as getting the gospel out because what might strike us as a theological error, muddling the gospel with the law, is, for Paul, a pastoral emergency.

Just game out the practical implications of the false teachers' glawspel message. The false teachers had convinced the Christians in Galatia that, by dint of their good-deed-doing, upright living, and button-down piety, they were the active agents of their salvation—a glad, flattering message so long as you're playing the game of life with a full house and an ace in the hole. But by that same logic, as soon as life deals you a few rotten hands or you go bust-up and broke, it's your fault. It's because of some sin you committed or some commandment you did not keep.

It's the logic of the law.

If/then. Merit and demerit. Reward and punishment. Karma.

But the church is a hospital for sinners.

The church is a hospital for sinners, and the Letter to the Galatians is Paul, wearing a surgical gown and tethered to an IV pole, screaming, "But you can't sell this in a hospital! You can't sell this to me!" There is perhaps no surer evidence that God does not operate according to a system of merit and demerit than the assumption that lies behind Paul's command in our text today, "Bear one another's burdens, in this way you fulfill the law of Christ." That the community of disciples are commanded to share one another's hardships and suffering is but an indication that hardships and suffering are inevitable.

God's people are not to think themselves exempt from hardship. Indeed God's people are commanded to expect hardship and, in the face of hardship, they are commanded not to allow one another to suffer it alone. It's not that God sends hardship and suffering upon his people, but rather, in a world of hardship and suffering, God sends a people, a people called church, who bear one another's burdens.

Notice, moreover, Paul does not prescribe any words for us to offer one another in the course of our burden-bearing. Paul does not say "bear one another's burdens, reminding each other that all things work together for good." Paul does not say "bear each other's burdens, encouraging one another that everything happens for a reason." Paul only mentions speech in these verses when he tells us we're obligated to confront, in gentleness and truth, those who've trespassed against us. But Paul does not provide any words that should attend our burden-bearing.

It's like Paul knows we cannot be trusted with words in the face of suffering.

We're simply to be present to and share in one another's suffering, which is but a reminder that the God of the Bible has steadfastly refused to give us any explanation for the persistence of suffering in the world. Rather than an explanation for suffering, what God has given a suffering world is a community of care made possible by his cross, a people whose practice of bearing one another's burdens, Paul says, fulfills the law.

Thomas Lynch is a poet and an undertaker in Milford, Michigan. In his book of essays, *The Undertaking: Life Studies from the Dismal Trade*, Lynch reflects on bearing one another's burdens as he writes about preparing the body of his dead friend, Milo Hornsby:

Last Monday morning Milo Hornsby died. Mrs. Hornsby called at 2 a.m. to say that Milo had expired and would I take care of it, as if his condition were like any other that could be renewed or somehow improved upon. At 2 a.m., yanked from my REM sleep, I am thinking, put a quarter into Milo and call me in the morning. But Milo is dead. Milo is dead. In the hospital where he died, Milo is downstairs, between SHIPPING & RECEIVING and LAUNDRY ROOM, in a stainless-steel drawer, wrapped in white plastic top to toe. I sign for him and get him out of there. Back at the funeral home, upstairs in the embalming room, behind a door marked PRIVATE, I shave him, close his eyes, his mouth. We call this setting the features. These are the features, eyes and mouth, that will never look the way they would have looked in life when they were always opening, closing, focusing, signaling, telling us something. In death, what they tell us is that they will not be doing anything anymore. The last detail to be managed is Milo's hands, one folded over the other, over the umbilicus, in an attitude of ease, of repose, of retirement. They will not be doing anything anymore, either. When my wife moved out some years ago, the children stayed here with me, as did the dirty laundry. It was big news in a small town. There was the gossip and the goodwill that places like this are famous for. And while there was plenty of talk, no one knew exactly what to say to me. They felt helpless, I suppose. So they brought casseroles and beef stews, took the kids out to the movies or canoeing, brought their younger sisters around to visit me.

What Milo did was send his laundry van around twice a week for two months, until I found a housekeeper. Milo would pick up five loads in the morning and return them by lunchtime, fresh and folded. I never asked him to do this. I hardly knew him. I had never been in his home or his laundromat. His wife had never known my wife. His children were too old to play with my children. After my housekeeper was installed, I went to thank Milo and pay the bill. The invoices detailed the number of loads, the washers and the dryers, detergent, bleaches, fabric softeners. When I asked Milo what the charges were for pick-up and delivery, for stacking and folding and sorting by size, for saving my life and the lives of my children, for keeping us in clean clothes and towels and bed linen, "Never mind that," is what Milo said. "One hand washes the other," is what Milo said.

I place Milo's right hand over his left hand, then try the other way. Then back again. Then I decide that it doesn't matter. One hand washes the other either way.[2]

2. Lynch, *Undertaking*, 9.

By bearing one another's burdens we fulfill the law of Christ. That's a remarkable statement. How? How does our sharing in one another's suffering, being present amidst another's pain, fulfill the intent of the law? The law of Christ, Jesus makes clear in the Gospels, is consonant with the law of Moses. "Do not think that I have come to abolish the law or the prophets"; Jesus preaches in the Sermon on the Mount, "I have not come to abolish them but to fulfill them. For truly, I say to you, until heaven and earth pass away, not one jot or tittle will pass from the law." The law of Christ, Christ makes clear, accords with the law of Moses. The purpose of the law of Moses was for God's particular people, Israel, to be a light to the nations. To bear witness to the wider world that this is what life with God looks like. To live already as a harbinger of a kingdom not yet come. But how? How does our taking the time to suffer the presence of another who suffers constitute a light to the nations?

I visit the oncologist every month for blood work and scans and "maintenance chemo," a euphemism meant to mask the brute fact that what we're maintaining is my life. My doctor has the appearance of a Bond villain and, even better, the bedside manner of an East German Stasi interrogator. For every visit, he repeats what I remember him doing the first time I woke up from surgery a few years ago to the news that I had a rare, incurable form of cancer. Each time, he flips over the nearest box of tissues or rubber gloves and in thick, black lines drawn with a sharpie he sketches out the bell curve for the standard deviation of the time I've likely got left.

I think it was the third of fourth time, sitting on butcher paper and staring at the bell curve like it was the hourglass from *Days of Our Lives,* the truth swept over me like forced sobriety. Life is made up of minutes, not moments. Life is not made up of moments but minutes. It's a treasure all of us possess only in ever-increasing poverty. And then, almost immediately, a second realization struck me. That life is made up of minutes not moments was also true of every fellow believer and church member who had taken the time to pray for me or visit me or cook for me, every person who accompanied me to chemo infusions or caught me when those infusions left me teetering. Their lives too were made up of minutes, not moments, yet they had wasted their time on me. Rather than seizing their own day or checking off a bucket list of their own, instead of a more fulfilling activity—because, YOLO—or living their own best lives now, they'd joined me in my worst time.

Life is made up of minutes, not moments; nevertheless, God has called forth a people to waste precious time, lavishing it on the burdens of a brother or sister. This is the way in which our suffering the presence of the suffering other fulfills the law. This is the manner in which our bearing one another's burdens in turn bears witness to the world, for the world is determined by a fear of scarcity—especially the scarcity of time. I mean, some are willing to let the planet get hotter and hotter in the belief that the time we have right now is the only time we have, so damn the future. Such fear informs our economic unrest. Such fear feeds the anger and grievance in our politics. Such fear produces the sense of urgency and anxiety that besets our institutions, particularly the church. We're running out of time to recover what we had in the past. In such a world, a world determined by the conviction that time is a commodity with shrinking returns, God has called a people to take the time out of their own shrinking treasury of time to suffer the presence of those who suffer.

It's true, of course, that many people bear the burdens of others. A willingness to bear the burdens of another is not necessarily an indication that you're a Christian. However, only Christians are commanded to bear the burdens of one another, and only Christians are told that so doing summarizes the entire vocation of God's people to be a light to the nations. In other words—Christians and non-Christians alike may bear the burdens of others; in fact, many non-Christians may perform the work of burden-bearing better than Christians. That burden-bearing summarizes our vocation means that what the Christian possesses that the non-Christian lacks is a particular story that makes intelligible our willingness to waste our time on the pain and suffering of others. We have a narrative—a promise—that can account for our willingness to spend our minutes on someone whose pain we cannot remove and whose problems we cannot solve.

To bear the burdens of another, therefore, is to live in a manner that suggests our story is true. Life is not finished, even when it is over. There will be more moments to follow our allotment of minutes, because the tomb is empty. He is not there. He has been raised. He has gone ahead of us. And, in the fullness of time, he will come again and raise you up to a new, renewed time. And, therefore, you have an abundance of time—literally all the time—out of which you can afford to live your neighbor's worst life now. You can so afford to live because, on the contrary, you do not only live once.

Cruciform Calisthenics

I N HIS BOOK, *Two Cheers for Anarchism*, the political philosopher James Scott tells a story of a sabbatical he took in Germany during which he attempted to learn to speak better German by interacting with pedestrians in the street, shoppers in stores, and waitstaff at cafes and bars. Scott reflects upon one afternoon in a small German city in which he observed pedestrians at an intersection near the train station. A traffic light signaled for pedestrians when it was legal and when it was not legal to cross the street. When Scott walked up to the intersection, he noticed that the entire group of sixty to seventy-five pedestrians waited in obedience to the traffic light even though no cars were to be seen on the small-town road.

Intrigued, Scott decided to remain at the intersection and investigate. After over five hours of observation, Scott reports that he saw not more than two people—out of several hundred—disobey the traffic signal in order to cross an empty street. Moreover, those two pedestrians who did disobey the traffic light and unlawfully cross the intersection received scornful looks and reproachful comments from their fellow pedestrians. Scott comments that he had to screw up his courage and risk the crowd's contempt by crossing against the traffic light in order finally to catch his train on time. He justified his law-breaking performance, he notes, by telling himself that his German-Christian grandparents could have used more of a spirit of law-breaking in the name of justice. But because his grandparents' generation had lost the practice of breaking small laws, Scott writes, they no longer possessed the discipline to recognize when it truly mattered to break more meaningful laws; that is, they lacked the discipline to suffer the reproach of their fellow citizens. Scott refers to this practice of small law-breaking and discrete acts of disobedience as anarchist calisthenics, and he observes that the Germans could've used a hell of a lot more anarchist calisthenics in the 1930s.

We all feel the urge to conform; it is the most normal of human desires. It goes against our nature to go against the crowd.

"See what large letters I make when I am writing in my own hand! It is those who want to make a good showing in the flesh that try to compel you to be circumcised—only that they may not be persecuted for the cross of Christ." Throughout his Letter to the Romans, the apostle Paul personifies such terms as sin and death, making them the subjects of verbs as though they have an agency in the world of their own. In a similar manner, Paul speaks of the law as though it were an enslaving adversary and writes, mysteriously, of the powers. It's not until the close of his epistle that Paul pulls back the curtain and reveals to whom all of these auspicious terms point. At the end of Romans 16, Paul announces, "The God of peace will in due season crush Satan under your feet." Romans needs to be read backwards in order for Paul's letter to come into clear focus. Likewise, it's only at the end of his angry diatribe against the false teachers in Galatia, declaring anathema anyone who would add the law back on to the gospel, that the apostle Paul makes plain the problem that has produced the false teachers' counterfeit gospel. "See what large letters I make when I am writing in my own hand!" Paul writes in verse 11; in other words, what's to follow is the all-caps, underlined takeaway from his email to the Galatians.

"It is those who want to make a good showing in the flesh that try to compel you to be circumcised in order that they may not be persecuted for the cross of Christ." It's not simply about self-justification; it's about self-preservation. It's only here, at the end of his letter, that Paul spells it out in fifty-point font. The false teachers are compelling believers in Christ to go back to Moses for the purpose of avoiding the persecution of the cross. The motivation for their ersatz message is evasion. With their false gospel, they hope to sidestep the suffering that might attend the true gospel.

Persecution from whom? And how?

We know from Pliny the Younger's letters to the emperor that Rome at the time of Paul's Letter to the Galatians regarded Christians as little more than an odd burial society. The church wasn't yet in Caesar's crosshairs; furthermore, Rome had no stake in whether or not this insignificant band of Jesus-followers underwent circumcision or made the law of Moses a necessary component of their gospel. Jewish persecution is the only kind of persecution circumcision and law would help you avoid.

Remember, in the first century, every Christian was either a convert from paganism or a convert from Judaism. And everywhere outside of

Jerusalem the body of Christ was comprised of both gentile Christians and Jewish Christians, of whom the latter insisted the former should have to undergo circumcision and follow Torah. They need to become like us. Because Christ died for all, the logic of the cross demands that the church show solidarity with gentiles, who previously were regarded by God's people with contempt and suspicion. "In Christ Jesus," Paul has already argued, "you are all children of God through faith. As many of you as were baptized into Christ have clothed yourselves with Christ. There is no longer Jew or Gentile; for all of you are one in Christ Jesus."

The implications of the cross are such that these preachers should stand in solidarity with the gentiles, requiring nothing of them but faith in Christ, but they are not willing to suffer the consequences of their convictions. The false teachers added the law back onto the gospel in an attempt to avoid suffering for the sake of their gentile neighbors. Rather than provoke the reproach of their nongentile neighbors, they opted to preach "a different gospel which is no gospel at all."

It's not surprising.

It goes against our nature to go against the crowd. We all feel the urge to conform. It is the most normal of human desires.

John Archibald is a Pulitzer Prize–winning journalist for the *Birmingham News*. He grew up in Alabama, the son of a successful Methodist minister, Rev. Bob Archibald, during the most turbulent years of the Civil Rights movement. However, John Archibald did not know he was growing up during the turmoil of the Civil Rights Movement because his father, the reverend Bob Archibald, assiduously avoided any mention of the struggle for racial justice. Having been a public school student in Birmingham and later a history major at the University of Alabama, the first time John Archibald ever read Martin Luther King Jr.'s "Letter from a Birmingham Jail" was when he started working as a metro reporter for the *Birmingham News* and wanted to learn more about the city. He writes:

> I was born in the midst of revolution. The son of a preacher, the grandson of preachers. The great-grandson of preachers, too. They preached on horseback and on foot and—in my dad's case—in a little white Fiat Spider. They preached of right and wrong and grace and goodness and believed it, I think, to their bones. In the name of God and something they called sanctifying grace, they preached in the Old South and longed for a New South, but were

silent, too silent, on the complicit and conspiratorial South I never came to see until I was fully grown.[1]

Only when he began work as a reporter for the *Birmingham News*—in 1986—did Archibald discover that Dr. King's letter, like Paul's own letter, was intended to rebuke false teachers; in King's case, the letter was a rebuke of white moderate preachers like Bob Archibald:

> The point of the letter was the rebuke. For retreat, in the name of peace. For obedience, in the name of law. For silence, in the voice of God. The point of the letter was shame and disappointment, and a truth so deep and ingrained that some people look at it for a lifetime and never see it at all. The point of this letter was not a message to Black people. It was a message to cautious and careful white people, like the members of my family, who thought they understood. It was to people just like mine, who tried to live like Jesus but turned the other cheek only to look away.[2]

In his book, *Shaking the Gates of Hell: A Search for Family and Truth in the Wake of the Civil Rights Revolution*, Archibald puts the journalistic spotlight on his father's ministry, examining the pages of his father's sermons alongside the pages of the newspaper, comparing what was happening in the South with what his father was preaching at the time. Rev. Archibald's sermon manuscripts exude the warmth and gentleness of a pastor rather than a preacher whose sermons "will shake the gates of hell" (John Wesley's definition of good preaching).

Reading his father's sermons, John Archibald wrestles with the realization that his father was the kind of preacher who in their modest, folksy Methodism, gave aid and comfort to a society that gave African-Americans hell. Rev. Bob Archibald was unwilling to upset his congregation, many of whom were his friends, with the truth and who therefore avoided suffering the persecution of the cross. For example, as Congress debated the Civil Rights Act, Rev. Archibald preached on snobbery. The Sunday after the Sixteenth Street Baptist Church was bombed, killing four little girls, Rev. Archibald stepped into the pulpit with a sermon bearing the ironic title, "Too Late."

John Archibald writes that, sadly, his father's sermon that Sunday was "a tepid treatise on missing the boat, which itself missed the boat."[3] The

1. Archibald, *Shaking the Gates of Hell*, 7.
2. Archibald, *Shaking the Gates of Hell*, 6.
3. Archibald, *Shaking the Gates of Hell*, 71.

Sunday after the Children's Crusade, as thousands of children sat jailed in Birmingham—arrested by Bull Connor, a Methodist in good standing—Rev. Archibald preached a sermon on having the trust of a child. Reflecting on his father's anodyne sermon, John Archibald writes,

> There was no mention of arrested children in that message, no acknowledgment of crusades and retribution, or protest, or inequality, or the fact that any of those things were in debate. There was only the notion that good Christians "must become like little children in many ways." But Christ means for us to be childlike not childish. Christians should be childlike in their candor, their willingness to speak truth without fear of offense, without counting of the cost of truthful speech.[4]

It goes against our nature to go against the crowd.

It's survival instinct.

It's hard to read Rev. Bob Archibald's sermons and not consider my own preaching. God, I think, I hope my sons never grow up to be journalists. The Sunday after George Floyd was murdered one of you called me on my cell phone later that afternoon to tear me a new one.

"I cannot believe you could preach as though nothing had happened. I'd be more likely to trust the church if there was just a hint in church of all the great and horrible things that were happening outside the church."

"Hey, cut me some slack. It's an online worship service. I recorded that sermon two weeks ago," I said truthfully.

But truthfully, when George Floyd was murdered and unrest was unleashed across the country, I was relieved to have already recorded my sermon, and I counted myself lucky that I was out of town that Sunday visiting my niece. When I did finally mention George Floyd in a sermon, I suggested that racism is a theological issue, and I said that the cross compels us to worry less about the feelings of white people like me, who know not what to do with our complex legacy as a genocidal slave nation, and to worry more about how with every George Floyd we attempt to explain away we crucify Christ anew.

The Monday after that Sunday I came to the office only to find a long, heated message waiting for me on my voicemail from a church member informing me they were leaving the church. Another voicemail bellowed that Black Lives Matter is a terrorist organization and wondered on what Sunday will I express my support for Hezbollah. Two other callers called to tell me

4. Archibald, *Shaking the Gates of Hell*, 58.

they would stop giving to the church. By the Tuesday after that Sunday I had received fourteen emails criticizing me bringing politics into the pulpit, half of those emails were from people outside the church who listen to the sermons from other parts of the country—people who, they told me in all caps and angry face emojis, would never listen again.

It almost made me wish I hadn't crossed the street against the light.

Even more unpleasant than the angry rebukes was my realization that my preaching has seldom been so faithful as to provoke reproach and hostility.

"From now on, let no one make trouble for me; for I carry the mark of Jesus branded on my body."

At the beginning of his Letter to the Galatians, Paul asserts his apostolic authority by appealing to his encounter with the Risen Christ. Now, at the end of his letter, Paul once again puts his foot down, but this time Paul points to the mark of Christ that Paul bears branded on his own body. It's true that Paul's preaching has led Paul's listeners to whip him with thirty-nine lashes on five different occasions. And three times Paul's hearers beat him with rods. Still another time, after Paul's sermon, they stoned him and left him for dead. But those bruises and smoothed-over scars are not what Paul's referring to when Paul refers to the mark of Christ branded on his body. Paul is instead harkening to the provision in the Torah, in the book of Deuteronomy (15:16), for emancipated slaves who nevertheless choose to remain bound as slaves to their master. Under the law such slaves who choose to remain slaves would be "branded," that is, they would be marked out by a hole pierced through their ear. To the false teachers in the churches throughout the region of Galatia, to those preachers who've diluted the word of the cross and concocted their own glawspel message as a means of conflict avoidance, to them the apostle Paul says finally, "I carry the mark of Jesus branded on my body."

In other words, I chose to be Christ's slave, so I'll take the consequences of my convictions. What did you think you were signing up for exactly? You don't have to be a Christian. Christians are made, not born. You have to be born again into this life. If you don't want this life, fine, but you can't have it both ways. Don't turn it into something it's not. There's simply no way of following the Crucified Jesus that doesn't require your readiness to carry the cross.

Notice how Paul speaks of the cross here at the end of his epistle. Paul does not speak of the cross as an episode in Christ's biography, nor as the necessary prelude to the empty grave. Paul speaks of the cross as significant in and of itself, yet Paul does not speak of the cross as a moment in the past, nor as an event for our sins. Here, at the end of his angry letter, Paul speaks of the cross as our stance toward the world. For Paul, the cross is our whole attitude in the world. Because Christ, the servant of all, died for all, there is no one with whom we are not in solidarity. Because the one who died for all is the LORD of all, we live as no other lord's subjects—even to the point of suffering the slings and scorns of our neighbors, especially even the neighbors who are our friends and family.

Christ's cross, Paul makes clear here at the end, was the price to pay for representing a new way of life in a world that did not want a new way of life. Not only does the world still not want his way of life, Jesus still stubbornly summons those he's called to take up their crosses and follow him.

What did you think you were signing up for? Perhaps you can't be held responsible for your confusion. After all, we no longer pierce ears to signify our slavery to the Crucified God. Instead, we baptize. I realize that it can sound daunting to proclaim the word of the cross and to follow Christ in a world that still prefers to crucify him. I understand that to suggest being a Christian necessarily entails the readiness to suffer for our convictions can seem impossibly overwhelming. I mean, who wants to tell the truth all the time about every circumstance, that it's on us to carry forward the cruciform way in the world? Look, I get it. But to the extent such a form of following frightens us, to the degree to which it seems daunting and overwhelming to live fully the implications of the cross in our world—that we would show solidarity with everyone and be the subject of no other LORD or power—to the extent discipleship frightens us, we betray our functional atheism.

Because we do not follow Jesus apart from Jesus.

God is not nowhere in our world.

Jesus never stopped forming his disciples to be a people in the world capable of making his way intelligible to the world. He's still forming his followers in a manner no less real than the way he formed Peter or James or John. God is not nowhere in the world. He's here, in bread and wine. He's in the water, with which earlier we baptized a little girl: Brynne. He's in the word, giving himself to us so that we might learn the wisdom and develop the discipline to cross against the light when the moment matters.

Bread and wine. Water and word.

Worship: it's a cruciform calisthenics.

It's training through which the Living Christ is forming us to be his truthful speech to the world. God is not nowhere in the world. He's here, in these creatures of bread and wine and water and word, summoning us still to take up our crosses, and forming us to be able to do so. Which means, even though it's against our nature to go against the crowd, because God is not dead—he's here, as real to you as he was to Peter or Andrew—it's never too late for us to disobey the light, to cross the street, to speak the truth, to suffer the consequences of our cross-shaped convictions.

For example, John Archibald, the journalist at the *Birmingham News*, his older brother, Murray, married a man named Steve in their church in Delaware in 2012. The couple had founded a ministry for LGBTQ youth in Rehobeth Beach. Seeing his son's faithful, monogamous, loving, costly relationship with Steve gave Rev. Bob Archibald the courage to speak out in defense of the full inclusion of gay and lesbian people in the United Methodist Church. At the 1992 General Conference of the United Methodist Church, "in front of all the Methodist preachers and laypeople who were quoting the Bible to condemn gays and lesbians and his own son," quiet, self-effacing Bob took to the floor and with a clear voice declared, "It is not a choice, and it is not a choice for us either. Jesus said to love. And love is unconditional."[5] When Rev. Bob Archibald returned to Alabama, he was condemned and threatened. "One preacher told him to his face that he had known the Archibald family for generations and had respect for all of them. 'Not anymore,' the man said. 'Not anymore.'"[6]

In his book, John Archibald reports that his father learned something in receiving the fierce, angry responses: "He found that it didn't bother him. It didn't bother him at all." Rev. Bob Archibald followed his witness at that General Conference with another one in 2019, writing a sardonic op-ed in his son's newspaper entitled, "Methodists Don't Let the Door Hit You on the Way Out." The preacher of that tone-deaf, people-pleasing, conflict-avoidant glawspel sermon "Too Late" had discovered that, because our Crucified LORD is very much alive, it's never too late to find your voice, cross the street, defy the light, or pick up a cross.

5. Archibald, *Shaking the Gates of Hell*, 256.
6. Archibald, *Shaking the Gates of Hell*, 221.

Bibliography

Archibald, John. *Shaking the Gates of Hell: A Search for Family and Truth in the Wake of the Civil Rights Revolution.* New York: Knopf, 2021.

Barth, Karl. *Commentary on the Epistle to the Romans.* Oxford: Oxford University Press, 1968.

———. *Deliverance to the Captives.* New York: Harper Collins, 1978.

Bonhoeffer, Dietrich. *Discipleship: Dietrich Bonhoeffer Works, Volume 4.* 13 vols. Minneapolis: Fortress, 2003.

Bowler, Kate. *No Cure for Being Human (And Other Truths I Need to Hear).* New York: Random House, 2021.

Busch, Eberhard. *Karl Barth: His Life from Letters and Autobiographical Texts.* Grand Rapids: Eerdmans, 1975.

Capon, Robert. *The Supper of the Lamb: A Culinary Reflection.* New York: The Modern Library, 2002.

Cavell, Stanley. *The Claim of Reason: Wittgenstein, Skepticism, Morality, and Tragedy.* Oxford: Oxford University Press, 1979.

Clifton, Shane. *Crippled Grace: Disability, Virtue Ethics, and the Good Life.* Waco, TX: Baylor University Press, 2018.

DeMille, Cecil B., dir. *The Ten Commandments.* Hollywood: Paramount, 1956.

Eliot, T. S. *The Four Quartets.* New York: Mariner, 1943.

Forde, Gerhard. On *Being a Theologian of the Cross: Reflections on Luther's Heidelberg Disputation.* Grand Rapids: Eerdmans, 1997.

Hallie, Phillip. *Lest Innocent Blood Be Shed: The Story of the Village of Le Chambon and How Goodness Happened There.* New York: Harper Collins, 1979.

Hauerwas, Stanley. *Fully Alive: The Apocalyptic Humanism of Karl Barth.* Charlottesville: The University of Virginia Press, 2022.

———. *Minding the Web: Making Theological Connections.* Eugene, OR: Cascade, 2018.

Holland, Tom. *Dominion: How the Christian Revolution Remade the World.* New York: Basic, 2019.

Langston, Katie. *Sealed: An Unexpected Journey into the Heart of Grace.* St. Paul: Thornbush, 2021.

Luther, Martin, *The Freedom of a Christian, 1520: The Annotated Luther Study Edition.* Minneapolis: Fortress, 2016.

———. *Luther's Large Catechism.* St. Louis: Concordia, 1978.

———. *Luther's Works: Volume 24: Lectures on Galatians: Chapters 1-4.* 48 vols. Minneapolis: Fortress, 1962.

Lynch, Thomas. *The Undertaking: Life Studies from the Dismal Trade.* New York: Penguin, 1997.

McClendon, James. *Biography as Theology: How Life Stories Can Remake Today's Theology.* Reprint, Eugene, OR: Wipf and Stock, 2002.

Micheli, Jason. *Cancer Is Funny: Keeping Faith in Stage-Serious Cancer.* Minneapolis: Fortress, 2016.

Migliore, Daniel. *Reading the Gospels with Karl Barth.* Grand Rapids: Eerdmans, 2017.

Rousseau, Jean-Jacques. *The Major Political Writings of Jean-Jacques Rousseau: The Two "Discourses" and the "Social Contract."* Chicago: University of Chicago Press, 2014.

Rutledge, Fleming. *And God Spoke to Abraham: Preaching from the Old Testament.* Grand Rapids: Eerdmans, 2011.

Sayers, Dorothy L. *Creed or Chaos?: Why Christians Must Choose Either Dogma or Disaster; Or, Why It Really Does Matter What You Believe.* Nashua, NH: Sophia Institute, 1995.

Steinbuch, Yaron. "Professor Resigns after Student Refuses to Wear Mask Correctly." *New York Post*, August 30, 2021. https://nypost.com/2021/08/30/university-of-georgia-professor-resigns-after-student-refuses-to-wear-mask-correctly/.

Stott, John. *Between Two Worlds: The Challenge of Preaching Today.* Grand Rapids: Eerdmans, 1982.

———. *The Cross of Christ.* Downers Grove, IL: InterVarsity, 1986.

———. *The Message of Galatians.* The Bible Speaks Today Series. Downers Grove, IL: Intervarsity, 1968.

Tolkien, J. R. R. *The Fellowship of the Ring.* New York: Harper Collins, 1988.

Wengert, Timothy. *The Freedom of a Christian 1520: The Annotated Luther Study Edition.* Minneapolis: Fortress, 2016.

Williams, Rowan. *The Truce of God.* Grand Rapids: Eerdmans, 2005.

Willimon, Will. *Accidental Preacher: A Memoir.* Grand Rapids: Eerdmans, 2019.

9 781666 744514